WE CAN OVERCOME

WE CAN OVERCOME

AN AMERICAN BLACK CONSERVATIVE MANIFESTO

Lt. Col. ALLEN B. WEST (Ret.)

BROWN BOOKS
PUBLISHING GROUP

We Can Overcome
An American Black Conservative Manifesto

Brown Books Publishing Group
Dallas, TX / New York, NY
www.BrownBooks.com
(972) 381-0009

A New Era in Publishing®

Publisher's Cataloging-In-Publication Data

Names: West, Allen, 1961- author.
Title: We can overcome : an American Black conservative manifesto / Lt. Col. Allen B. West (Ret.).
Description: Dallas, TX ; New York, NY : Brown Books Publishing Group, [2020] | Includes bibliographical references.
Identifiers: ISBN 9781612544335
Subjects: LCSH: Conservatism--United States. | African Americans--Politics and government. | African American families--United States. | United States--Race relations--Political aspects. | African Americans--Social conditions.
Classification: LCC JC573.2.U6 W47 2020 | DDC 320.520973--dc23

ISBN 978-1-61254-433-5
LCCN 2019912549

Printed in the United States
10 9 8 7 6 5 4 3 2 1

Pictured on the cover: Booker T. Washington, Second Lieutenant Henry O. Flipper, Frederick Douglass, Thomas Sowell, and Madam C. J. Walker

For more information or to contact the author, please go to www.TheOldSchoolPatriot.com.

This book is dedicated to two black men. First, my ideological mentor, Booker T. Washington. He will always be, to me, the father of black conservatism. Washington is a role model whose exemplary rise up from slavery should be an inspiration to us all. He knew that education is the great equalizer, and his philosophy is one that can restore not just the American black community, but America as a whole.

Secondly, I would like to dedicate this book to the first black commissioned officer in our US Army, United States Military Academy graduate, Second Lieutenant Henry O. Flipper. Without his perseverance, it may not have been possible for subsequent generations, including myself, to follow in his footsteps as proud American black commissioned military officers.

Booker T. Washington, Henry O. Flipper—
you gave us a blueprint and a roadmap to show how we can overcome.

CONTENTS

PART I
OUR ROOTS, OUR HISTORY, OUR FIRST PRINCIPLES

PART II
OUR HISTORY FROM EXECUTIVE ORDER 9981
TO THE COMMUNITY REINVESTMENT ACT

PART III
TWENTY-FIRST CENTURY ECONOMIC PLANTATION

PART IV
THE FUTURE FOR THE AMERICAN BLACK COMMUNITY

INTRODUCTION

I was born on February 7, 1961, at Atlanta's Hughes Spalding Hospital. I often tell folks that you cannot get more Atlanta than someone like myself, born in the Grady hospital system and a graduate of Henry W. Grady High School. The only thing missing from the ultimate trifecta would have been growing up in Grady Homes. Back in 1961, when I came into the world, Hughes Spalding Hospital was specifically for blacks. Today, of course, that is no longer the case, as it is a children's health-care facility. Some things, such as the hospital, have changed for the better; other things in the black community have changed for the worse.

I am truly blessed—no, honored—to be able to say that I grew up in Atlanta's historic Old Fourth Ward neighborhood. What makes the Fourth Ward so historic? Well, simple: it was the home of Dr. Martin Luther King Jr. Yes, he was born and raised there also. Auburn Avenue in Old Fourth Ward was the home of the black civil rights movement and is where Dr. King and his wife Coretta Scott King were laid to rest. The headquarters of the Southern Christian Leadership Council was also on Auburn Avenue, along with a multitude of black-owned businesses and the professional offices of doctors (such as mine, Dr. Harper) and lawyers.

Right off Auburn Avenue is a little street called Butler. There sits the historic Butler Street YMCA, the place where I perfected my basketball game and learned to swim and box. At the intersection of Boulevard Avenue and Auburn Avenue was my elementary school, Our Lady of Lourdes Catholic. Our Lady of Lourdes is the oldest black Catholic parish in Atlanta. I even have a copy of my fifth-grade class photo on my cell phone. My elementary school is no more; it is just a community center now. Like I said, some things have not changed for the better.

I grew up with two awesome parents, Herman "Buck" West and Elizabeth Thomas "Snooks" West. I tell much of their story in my first book, *Guardian of the Republic*. If anyone wants to know where my fundamental principles, values, and convictions came from, well, ya can thank ol' Buck and Snooks. Dad was a World War II veteran and Mom served for more than twenty-five years with an army recruiting command and the Sixth Marine Corps District headquarters. They are buried together in Marietta National Cemetery. As they were in life, so they are in death: one man and one woman.

From my mom and dad, I learned so many important maxims and ol' sayings that have shaped my life, such as "never read your own press, and never drink your own tub water," "a hit dog will holler," and the best one: "never let your skin color be seen as an obstacle." They were echoing the famous words from Dr. King's "I Have a Dream" speech, in which he hoped for a nation where his children would be judged by the content of their character rather than the color of their skin.

My parents were registered Democrats—John Lewis was my congressional representative growing up—but the values of my parents were faith, family, individual responsibility, education, and service to our nation. My mom and dad decided not to send me to the community public schools, C. W. Hill and John Hope. As I mentioned before, their choice was to send me to Our Lady of Lourdes Catholic School, even though we were congregants at Fort Street United Methodist Church on Boulevard Avenue. They knew early on that education is indeed the great equalizer that opens to the equality of opportunity.

Mom and Dad had big dreams, and that is why they left southern Georgia and moved to Atlanta in 1959. Dad bought a home on 651 Kennesaw Avenue NE; it was $19,000. I will never forget the day when ol' Buck West made that final mortgage payment. Mom and Dad were truly owners of their own home, and to this day, I have always sought to own my own home, not rent. But it was there on those steps that

Corporal Herman West Sr. told me, his middle son, "There is no greater honor than wearing the uniform of the United States, and that is why I want you to be the first officer in our family."

See, my elder brother, Herman Jr., had enlisted—not been drafted, enlisted—in the US Marine Corps and served as an infantryman in Vietnam. He, like my dad in World War II, was wounded in combat at a place called Khe Sanh and left the corps as a lance corporal. Mom and Dad wanted something greater for their middle boy, and I was committed to fulfilling their dream and achieving my aspiration. And it happened, on July 31, 1982, at the University of Tennessee, Knoxville in the old Stokely Athletic Center; they pinned on my gold bars, making me a second lieutenant in the US Army. A proud day for Buck and Snooks.

One of my favorite stories to tell about my mom is from when I was playing high school football. See, Mom was a true southern woman; she loved sports and was not about raising any baby boy. Back in the day, there was no such thing as targeting in football; matter of fact, if you didn't try to clock a guy headfirst, you were considered a wussy. Well, I had a little reputation as a vicious hitter, and in one game I set my sights on a running back. We were like two rams hitting head to head. Yep, I got him, but the collision left me woozy—dazed and confused, as the Led Zeppelin song goes. I came to my senses on the sideline after several engagements with "smelling sauce" (more like skunk juice). I heard a faint voice in my ear, a familiar tone: my mom's soft, sweet southern accent. She had come down out of the stands. She was not screaming or hysterical; she was rather calm—although she did have a serious temper. I will never forget her whispering softly, "Allen, are you OK?"

After more blinks of the eyes, I replied, "Yeah, Mom, I am all right."

Mom's response was classic: "Well, baby, next time, you gotta wrap him up when you tackle him, your tackle form was terrible, OK?" All I know is that I said, "Yes, Mom!" and got back into the game. Why is that little anecdote so important? Simple: because my folks taught me that the measure of a man is not how many times he gets knocked down but how many times he gets back up!

As I look back on my early upbringing, I also reflect on what has happened in the black community. As stated, there are some things that have changed for the better, like Hughes Spalding Hospital, but much has changed for the worse.

The traditional two-parent black household has been decimated. When I was born, more than 70 percent of black kids nationally had a mom and a dad in the home; today, it is closer to 24 percent.[1] On Kennesaw Avenue, where I grew up, and replicated throughout the Old Fourth Ward, black families owned the homes where their children were raised. On Sunday morning, you could see scores of us boys and girls walking to our respective churches for Sunday school. Even at the historic Butler Street YMCA, Saturday started with Bible study before the gym and pool were open—and Bible study was highly attended.

Yes, we had our street gangs, but they were centered on who had the best street basketball team and who could rule the courts. Us boys wanted bikes, cap guns, and bench press sets for Christmas, and the police officers were our friends. Matter of fact, the day my elder brother drove his Atlanta Police Department patrol car up Kennesaw Avenue, all my friends came out to see. I was a proud younger brother; my big brother was a marine who had fought in combat, and now he was an Atlanta police officer!

Walking down Auburn Avenue and on Boulevard, I saw black-owned businesses and professionals. Sometimes my mom would make me walk all the way over to Bronner Brothers to get her hair products, and I would run part of the way because I wanted to be in good physical shape. Yes; as a little boy, I could walk the streets without fear of being shot.

Back then, we listened to WAOK and WIGO, two black-owned radio stations, and the music they played could be listened to by anyone.

There was no profanity, no bleeping, and the lyrics never disrespected black women or girls; nor did they promote black-on-black violence. Heck, who doesn't remember rapping along with the Sugarhill Gang to "Rapper's Delight"? And speaking of respecting black women and girls, having a baby out of wedlock was verboten—that's German for "frowned upon big time." The present phenomenon of girls having multiple babies out of wedlock and getting "gubmint checks" was not in the fabric of my upbringing—and I grew up in an inner-city community. And someone killing their unborn child? Nah; we respected life, and fellas were man enough to own up to their responsibilities. After all, it was all about family.

For us growing up, freedom was all about not owing anyone but having your own. Matter of fact, it was very common for kids who lived with their parents in their own homes to mock those kids who lived in government housing. Ya know, it was a pride thing; it was better to work and have your own than wait upon that gubmint check.

And yes, as teenagers, we worked part-time jobs. I started off at Baskin-Robbins in Ansley Mall before I got that coveted job at the Sears and Roebuck southeastern distribution center, which was right behind my house. Let me tell ya, that $3.25 minimum-wage job meant the world to me. It was about personal and fiscal responsibility as well as accountability. I was earning my own, and I was not looking for a living wage. I just wanted to be able to fill up the car with gas when my dad would allow me to drive it so that I could go to the movies and take my girlfriend out. You were big time when you could reach into your *own* pocket and pull out the bills—and I also learned to budget. My folks abhorred being in debt; they bought their cars in cash and used layaway—remember that—because they despised credit.

There are many who will try to attribute today's social issues in the black community to slavery and racism. However, how does one explain the fact—which is the truth—that many of these ills did not exist during the worst of times for the black community, segregation? Remember, I was born in a blacks-only hospital.

Much of what we are witnessing today can be traced to post–Great Society social welfare programs and policies. How has it been that a community that fought hard to raise victors is now struggling with those who see themselves as victims? The history of black America is inconsistent with what we see happening today. We must ask ourselves: What happened? Where was the turning point?

MY AMERICAN BLACK CONSERVATIVE MANIFESTO

The purpose of this literary endeavor is to historically articulate the principles, values, and foundations of the black community, tracing the steps from slavery to the Black Lives Matter movement and highlighting the people and events that proved to be pivotal to the history of the black America.

I intend to advocate not for a political party alignment but for the return of the black community to its founding principles: family union and values; education as a pivotal strategy for moving upward and onward; the independent and entrepreneurial mind-set of the black businessperson; selfless military service to defend the core principles of our country; and respect for authorities.

This book will place emphasis on the teachings and philosophies of our black predecessors. First among them is Booker T. Washington, born a slave in Virginia, as he explained in his 1901 autobiography *Up From Slavery*. He understood the value and power of self-improvement and professed the importance of uplifting the people through education—especially job training that allowed black youths to become skillful and employable workers. He urged the black community to learn a skill, distinguish themselves by working hard, and improve their quality of life by saving money and becoming property owners—a philosophy my parents proudly applied to their life.

After attending the Hampton Institute in Virginia, a school he arrived at with only fifty cents in his pocket, he established the Tuskegee Institute in Alabama. His nonconfrontational and indirect approach toward the widespread racial inequality suited the white community. As a result, many wealthy white people, such as John D. Rockefeller Jr., perceived Washington as a nonbelligerent and educated black man and were happy to financially help and support his projects.

While Washington preached a gradual and accommodating economic approach to the improvement and advancement of the black community, W. E. B. Du Bois—born a free man—ignited the fire in them with militant dialectic that admonished Washington's placid tones and accused him of worsening economic and racial disparities with the white community. In *The Souls of Black Folk*, his collection of essays published in 1903, Du Bois urged the black community to stop being submissive and start fighting for civil rights and for full citizenship rights. He highlighted the importance of a college education for black youth—he himself had a PhD in history from Harvard University—as the primary way for them to become leaders.

Even though these two leaders presented two different philosophies, their ultimate goal was the same: allow blacks to become strong, independent, first-class citizens of the country they helped build.

Our history in America is not of being victims; it is of being victors, even in the harshest of conditions. It is time we stop singing "We Shall Overcome" and assess the means by which we *can* overcome. Our predecessors gave us the keys, and it is time we found them again.

This book is my American black conservative manifesto. An attempt to restore the true-north principles of the American black community. I believe that we can overcome, but it will require us to go back to the ways, perspectives, and teachings of the ol' folks who fought to bring us out of physical bondage and enslavement—but not to see us weighed down by the metaphysical chains of economic enslavement.

My hometown Atlanta Falcons have a saying that is appropriate for this moment: Rise up!

Lt. Col. Allen B. West (US Army, Ret.)

Member, 112th US Congress

Proud son of Buck and Snooks West and product of the Old Fourth Ward neighborhood

PART I

OUR ROOTS, OUR HISTORY, OUR FIRST PRINCIPLES

CHAPTER ONE

THE FOUNDATIONS OF THE ENSLAVED BLACK COMMUNITY

The history of the black community in what would eventually become the United States of America begins with slavery. This is where we find our roots. But this is also where we find our founding principles and core values: strength, determination, and perseverance.

From the very beginning, black people were regarded as the other. What is the other? It is the different. The inferior. The threat. The other is the binary opposition of the self, which is identified as the norm, the superior, the security. Slavery defined the self as white America and the other as black people. The other must be controlled by the self, and it shall never learn of its true power and value, or it could become the self's menace—one that might cause its doom.

Our forefathers—Booker T. Washington *in primis*—had to fight and prove that through hard work, self-reliance, and knowledge, we can become successful and thriving members of the bigger American self.

We fought for the basic rights to earn a living and protect our families. Eventually, we won them. Then we became pawns in a political fight for power. White liberals, sensing demographic changes, started promising gifts to us—which they ultimately could not afford and which eventually backfired in their impact on our family structures and economic prowess.

The gifts from white liberal Democrats, whom I'll call progressive socialists throughout this book, come from a dark, dark place. Today, in this election cycle, their gifts have become another form of political control used in lieu of slavery. They've discovered that these American descendants of slaves are still eagerly reaching for handouts from their masters. Why would they stop offering now?

But we are not second-class human beings. We are nobody's slaves. We are nobody's Negroes. We don't have to wait for a handout from the American self. We *are* the American self. We don't need reparations. And do you know why? Because nothing is free; everything comes at a cost to its recipient, and we've already paid our dues.

When you consider the business side of slavery and how our forefathers were regarded as inhuman—as mere dirty farm tools without souls—you can better understand the pervasive racism that existed and still exists today. America created a system to keep these black tools in check, careful at every turn to prevent them from knowing they had souls worthy of equality.

Slavery was horrific and inexcusable. Those that sanctioned and perpetuated it will have hell to pay on Judgment Day. Our black forefathers endured an inhumane war that arguably rivals any other faced in the history of mankind.

Our debate within the black community has never really been about whether or not slavery happened or how bad it was. There's no argument there and never has been. We waste time trying to one-up the other person by reciting facts about the sin of slavery. We all agree that there have been negative reverberations from slavery. Where we disagree is on how best to deal with those reverberations.

I am Allen B. West, and I'm conservative because it is the most militant step we as black people can take. I believe and stand for our forefathers' core values of hard work, self-reliance, and education. I believe in protecting and serving our country. I believe in family. And I believe it is time for us to put a stop to handouts, a stop to behaving like we belong in the other America.

Have you not read Solomon's warnings in Proverbs 23:1–3 (King James Version)? "When thou sittest to eat with a ruler, consider diligently what is before thee: And put a knife to thy throat, if thou be a man given to appetite. Be not desirous of his dainties: for they are deceitful meat."

I'm leery of the deceitful meat from progressive socialists running for offices as Democrats. I have my freedom, and after what my forefathers went through, I've lost my appetite for the king's food. Haven't you?

STOLEN BODIES ARRIVE ON THE SHORES

To fully comprehend our present—and figure out what to do to better it—we must take a look back at how we got here by tracing our steps to way before the United States of America was even a concept.

As far as I could gather from research, the stealing and trading of African bodies started in 1441 with Portuguese sailors. That was nearly two hundred years before the first twenty African slaves landed at Point Comfort in Jamestown, Virginia, in 1619. The Spanish, Portuguese, French, and Dutch were already involved in the bustling trade of black bodies in South America and the Caribbean. As soon as Spaniards started landing in the Americas regularly, they brought slaves with them.[1]

After the first slaves were delivered in 1502, Catholic clergy traded, bought, and sold Africans in Atlantic markets and forced them to labor on plantations, in mines, and in towns.[2]

In 1530, a Dominican bishop begged King Charles V to deregulate the African trade—which required a royal license—to allow colonists in Santo Domingo, Cuba, and Puerto Rico greater access to labor.[3]

Europe came to rely on what became known as the triangle trade.[4] Ships would leave Europe for the west coast of Africa, chockful of guns, ammunition, spices, liquor, and other commodities, to bargain with African partners. When they landed in Africa, European merchants set up forts and trading posts known as slave castles to serve as command centers and staging areas. War, famine, political instability, and other disputes among the diverse African ethnic groups fed the flow of slaves to the coast from as far as a thousand miles inland.[5]

When it was time to depart, the ships would be outfitted with slave decks to carry human cargo of three hundred to seven hundred people.[6]

Merchants increased cargoes by laying enslaved people on their sides, chest to back, with little more than a couple of feet of vertical space.[7] They were often branded for identification and stripped nude to make them easier to wash down and secure.

Then came the two- to four-month long trip along the Middle Passage, that brutal space across the Atlantic to New World colonies in the Caribbean and North America. Africans were shackled in pairs and stuffed in the bowels of the ships, where rats and insects roamed along floors covered in blood and human excrement.[8] During the course of the trip, living slaves were often shackled next to dead slaves who had succumbed to disease, hunger, or suicide. As much as 10 percent did not survive the Middle Passage.[9]

All told, upward of twenty million Africans are estimated to have been torn from their homelands in the slave trade.[10] Even still, no one is sure how many died in Africa during the wars to take captives to be traded onto ships.

The African people didn't consider themselves African. They were a segmented people from different areas of the continent. There were, for example, the Fulani people from West Africa, the Ibo people from southeastern Nigeria, and the Akan people from the southern part of Ghana. They all spoke completely different languages, such as Fula, Igbo, and Kwa.

The ship captains were aware of these differences. They purposefully placed people from different cultures together as a way to control the human cargo by confusing their ability to communicate with each other and forcing them to understand a European language.

Perhaps it is because of these different languages—and the widespread and preferred use of oral tradition in African cultures—that we had to wait many years before we had any firsthand written accounts of what life was like for our forefathers.

A DOCTOR'S DIARY

The first internationally best-selling slave narrative—an autobiographical account of a fugitive or former slave titled *The Interesting Narrative of the Life of Olaudah Equiano, Or Gustavus Vassa, The African*—was published in 1789. Our understanding of what actually happened during slavery before that is limited to information gathered from newspaper articles of the day, diaries, and depositions in court cases when slave deals ended in disagreements between the buyers and suppliers.

It is thanks to Dr. William Chancellor, who recorded in his diary the story I am about to report, that we are aware of one of the most famous and heart-wrenching examples of the inhumanity of slave travel, which occurred on a slave ship called the *Wolf.*

On May 13, 1751, the *New-York Gazette* announced that children, women, and men were to be sold from the *Wolf* slave ship at the Meal Market at 10:00 a.m. the following Friday. The *Wolf* initially left New York City in September 1749 and reached the African coast in mid-November. Competition among Dutch, English, Portuguese, French, and American slavers and shortages of healthy captives prolonged the journey. Captain Gurnay Wall patrolled the shore for fourteen months, hopping from port to port, trading rum and other goods for small numbers of people.[11]

Dozens of human beings were imprisoned belowdecks as the captain tried to fill every space. "We know we are destined to stay till we do purchase a full complement," said Dr. William Chancellor, the ship's surgeon.[12]

As the *Wolf* approached the coast of Africa, Dr. Chancellor wrote that water flowed freely into the ship during storms, which forced the crew to stand ankle deep belowdecks or risk being swept into the ocean. According to his diary, by May 1750 three dozen people were chained below the deck, many of whom were sick small children. The slaves were cramped for so long that several could not walk without assistance. Dr. Chancellor recorded their suffering and his anxieties.

To make matters worse, white northerners who wanted to purchase slaves began asking for children instead of adults, whom they feared would be too rebellious. "For this market they must be young, the younger the better if not quite children, those advanced in years will never do," the merchant John Watts advised Gedney Clarke in 1762.[13] "I should imagine a cargo of them not exceeding 30 (in total) might turn out at 50 pounds a head gross sales."

On May 29—a Tuesday evening, according to Dr. Chancellor's published diary—a five-year-old slave girl died on the *Wolf*.[14] Wednesday morning, the surgeon went below and "found a boy dead, at noon another, and in the afternoon another." Dr. Chancellor suspected that his medicines were too potent; the medicine he had brought onboard was intended for adults, and he did not predict the captain would have small children in need of his medications.

"This morning early found another of the boys dead," he wrote. "The sight was shocking to see likely boys floating overboard is a misery to all on board."

On June 5, he decided to examine the corpse of a three-year-old slave girl who died on the ship. During her autopsy, he "found in her intestines seven worms some of them 12 and 13 inches, roll'd up together in a bundle." On a Saturday, a third girl died.

Days later, on June 13, he autopsied a baby and witnessed her "stomach chock'd full" of worms. According to the doctor's records in his diary, two slaves were dying each week, and most of them were children. That pace continued through August. The crew tossed scores of human bodies into the water as the *Wolf* sailed along the African coast for more than a year.[15]

The *Wolf* finally ended its horrific—yet ordinary—voyage when it arrived at the New York harbor in 1751. According to Dr. Chancellor's diary, Captain Wall had purchased 147 people on the African coast, but the slave records of the ship's receiving agent report that only 66 arrived in New York City.

PICKING A GOOD ONE

As if their voyage hadn't been traumatic enough, if slaves survived the Middle Passage, they were washed, oiled, paraded, and branded with hot irons like cattle.[16]

From my research on slave trading in the South, the slave markets were really clusters of competing firms, each of which kept its own yard for keeping slaves, called a slave pen. In Walter Johnson's 1999 book *Soul by Soul*, he gives an inside look into the business of the antebellum slave market. Between September and May—the months that bounded the trading season—the streets in front of the pens were lined with slaves dressed in blue suits and calico dresses. Sometimes the slaves paced back and forth; sometimes they stood atop a small foot stand, visible over a crowd of fascinated onlookers.[17] As many as a hundred slaves might occupy a single block, overseen by a few slave traders whose businesses were advertised by the painted signs hanging overhead, bearing such messages as "T Hart, Slaves" or "Charles Lamarque and Co., Negroes."

In these markets, human beings were broken down into parts and recomposed as commodities. Inexperienced buyers typically took some-one along with them when they went to the slave market.[18] For example, it was common for doctors and friends to come to the market at the request of uncertain buyers. Experienced men would examine the lots of slaves for sale in the market, reading their bodies aloud and helping buyers select the healthiest among them.

Slaves in the market were advertised by their sex, racial designation, age, and skill, and they were lined out for sale according to height.[19] They were presented as physical specimens, but it was a business of artful de-ceit, as their traders worked to cover up any infirmities and deformities.

The self-proclaimed savvy slave buyers knew how to look past the shiny black skin, blue suits, and frilly dresses. In his book, Johnson records the advice Mississippi planter John Knight gave his father-in-law, who was in the market for new slaves. "The fact is," Knight wrote, "as to the character and disposition of all of the slaves sold by the traders, we know nothing whatever, the traders themselves being generally such liars. Buyers therefore can only judge the looks of the Negroes."

Buyers preferred darker people over lighter ones for work in their fields and lighter people over darker ones for skilled and domestic labor. Buyers really didn't have access to reliable information on exactly where the slaves came from, so they relied on skin color to make their expert assessments. It was here in the slave market that white men created an unscientific determination of a man's ability based on his pigment, as if skin color could be a sign of a deeper set of qualities and character.

To them, blackness determined physical vitality. Accounts by slave traders and buyers show that they were concerned with a slave's ability to be acclimated to their environment. In many accounts, there were statements saying the "blackest" slaves were the healthiest. Johnson quotes published writings in which Samuel Cartwright said, "All Negroes are not equally black—the blacker the stronger." And in advice to his father-in-law, John Knight said, "I must have if possible the jet black Negroes, they stand this climate the best."

Buyers ran their hands over the bodies of the slaves. They rubbed their muscles and pressed their joints and kneaded their flesh. They took slaves' fingers in their hands, working them back and forth to see if they were "capable of the quick motions necessary in picking cotton," according to the account of buyer Charles Ball.[20] Similar to the process of examining a horse, buyers also would pry open a slave's mouth and run their fingers along the gums and teeth.

The prime age for a slave laborer was between fifteen and twenty-five. Buyers favored men and would pay higher prices for taller slaves.

Premium slaves would look like "Edward," a man whom slave dealer Louis Caretta called "one of the best sales in the state." According to the man who sold him, Edward was "stout . . . he was black and looked fat." Those that worked with him previously said he was a "big, strong athletic fellow."[21]

Typically, the public examination process might take anywhere between fifteen minutes to a half hour, but the bargaining might stretch over three or four days.[22] White men gained social clout and prestige among other white men for being a "good judge of slaves" in the pens.[23]

I believe it is clear from these accounts that this is when the differentiation between the American self and the other began. This is when white America started telling us who we are, what we can become, and what we are supposed to do.

This was true then, and it is true today. When you accept the daily provisions from the white progressive socialists, allow them to tell you how to teach your children, allow them to forfeit your right to protect yourself, allow them to siphon wealth from your family, and allow them to emasculate your men and deprive them of being industrious, then you have placed your soul on the auctioning block for someone else to purchase.

This sickens me, and it is time to change. After all, our forefathers did rebel against the status quo, showing a pervasive conservative spirit, like the one that burns deep inside my soul.

OUR HISTORIC LOVE FOR FAMILY

History tells us that there were more than 250 documented shipboard revolts by slaves and more than 250 violent incidents initiated by slaves on land.[24] One of the more well-known revolts occurred in 1739 in South Carolina. Africans outnumbered whites by two to one. On Sunday morning, when their masters were at church, a group of slaves assembled along the Stono River near Charleston.[25] They broke into a firearms store, took weapons, raided and set fire to the plantations lining the river, and reportedly killed twenty-five white men and women.[26] The Stono Rebellion was quickly stamped out by white colonists who outnumbered and outgunned the slaves, but the rebellion is an example of the gritty, resilient spirit of black men and women.

Our black forefathers and foremothers who were slaves refused to acquiesce and surrender to the tyranny of physical enslavement. They understood, just as America's Founding Fathers did, that there comes a time when armed rebellion is necessary to protect and preserve individual liberty and freedom. And today, we—the black community—must rediscover that rebellious spirit against the philosophy of progressive socialism, which endeavors to create economic enslavement.

We showed our conservatism not only in fighting but also in love. Even though the slaves initially didn't share a language, they learned to trust one another.[27] Sometimes they would deliberately sabotage a particular slave trade so their families could stay together.

Two-thirds of a million interstate slave sales were made by traders in the decades before the Civil War. Of these, 25 percent involved the destruction of a first marriage, and 50 percent destroyed a nuclear family.[28] Many of these separated children under the age of thirteen from their parents—and this is only accounting for the interstate slave sales.

Thomas Jones, a slave, was recorded as remembering a conversation from his parents when he was young. "My dear parents . . . talked about our coming misery, and they lifted up their voices and wept aloud as they spoke of us being torn from them and sold off to the dreaded slave trader."[29] In another account, a slave reported, "I had a constant dread that Mrs. Moore would be in want of money and sell my dear wife. We constantly dreaded a final separation. Our affection for each other was very strong and this made us always apprehensive of a cruel parting."

Harriet Newby wrote to her husband, "Dear husband, you know not the trouble I see; the last two years has been a trouble dream to me.

It is said master is in want of money. If so, I know not what time he may sell me."[30]

Another former slave, named Benjamin West, described his decision to run away: "My master died and I heard that I was to be sold, which would separate me from my family, and knowing no law which would protect me, I came away."[31]

The escapees were typically men, because childcare made it difficult for women to take on that risk. In the years before 1850, when men were being exported from the Upper South in greater numbers than women, they found themselves in a situation where they really had nothing to lose by running away.[32]

In a story of a mother's love, former slave Moses Grandy remembered, "My mother often hid us in the woods to prevent master [from] selling us." At that time, they survived on wild berries they found in the woods and on potatoes and raw corn that other nearby slaves stashed away for them.[33] "After a time, the master would send word to her to come in, promising her he would not sell us." By enlisting the support of other slaves in the neighborhood and withholding her labor and that of her children, Grandy's mother postponed their sale.[34] Often, all that a slave could hope for was to find another buyer who lived nearby, so that they could preserve their family.

I won't say that the black community in the United States ever completely experienced the good ol' days. Our file cabinet of United States history is indexed by battles to keep our families together and, later, for equality of opportunity.

It's always been an uphill trudge, but the climb was paved with an expectant hope that future generations of black men and women would have a better life. If it were somehow possible to summon the dead and get their commentary on today's black community, I believe they would be hurt by how so many have squandered the opportunities for which they fought.

If our forefathers and foremothers were able to support and help one another even though they didn't speak the same language, why can't we be on the same page now that we do have a common language? If our forefathers and foremothers risked their lives to become free and independent, to stop being somebody's property, to stop being at somebody else's mercy, why are we still willing to accept handouts? If our forefathers and foremothers rebelled against the status quo of being the other and bore arms to defend their right to be part of the American self, why are we behaving as if we still don't belong?

CHAPTER TWO

THE POLITICAL PARTY SCHISM ON THE ISSUE OF SLAVERY

Slavery has always been America's sin. I am referring not just to the time when black people living in the United States of America were physically enslaved and forced to work on plantations; I am also referring to the current mental and economic enslavement we have been subjected to by the Democratic Party by believing them when they say we need handouts, trusting that they know better, and waiting for them to tell us who we are and what we deserve.

Slavery has a long history in this country, and even though it was more dominant in the South, much of the leadership and funding for it came from the North. Many of our most prestigious Ivy League schools—such as Harvard, Yale, and Brown—all had ties to slavery. Nicholas and John Brown, two of the founders of what became Brown University, were slave traders; Harvard Law School was endowed with money its founder earned from selling slaves for Antigua's cane fields; and Yale University relied on slave-trading profits for its first scholarships, endowed professorships, and library endowments.[1]

Craig Steven Wilder's 2013 book *Ebony and Ivy* uncovers the sticky web of business that slavery spread across Ivy League schools. The founding, financing, and development of higher education in the colonies were thoroughly intertwined with the economic and social forces that transformed West and Central Africa through the slave trade and devastated indigenous nations in the Americas.[2]

In a class with Harvard anatomist John Collins Warren, students erroneously learned that in terms of physical development and intellectual potential, black people sat at the bottom of humanity.[3] Harvard was a pillar of the antebellum racial order.

College graduates apprenticed under the slave traders of New England, the mid-Atlantic, and Europe. They then migrated to the South and to the West Indies for careers as teachers, ministers, lawyers, doctors, politicians, merchants, and planters.

Even as slavery moved to the South, the end of the slave trade and the decline of slavery in the North did not break these ties.[4] In his book, Wilder shows how the antebellum South represented a field of opportunity where the wealth of the cotton planters funded the expansion of the educational infrastructure.

An education in Hartford or Cambridge was reasonable preparation for living among the slaveholders of Alabama. New England's colonizationists cast black slaves as a threat to democracy and social order, encouraged campaigns to halt the development of free black communities, and even destroyed schools for black children.[5] New England leaders attacked abolitionism as the cause of political tensions between the slave and free states.[6]

That's when tensions began to rise.

SLAVERY'S DEMAND CURVE

At the end of the eighteenth century, the slave trade started to follow the international demand curve for cotton. Slaves continued to cultivate tobacco, rice, and indigo, but with the invention of the cotton gin in 1793, the purchase of Louisiana in 1803, and the removal of the Native Americans, new regions of the South were opened up for cotton.[7]

By the 1830s, the price of slaves was so much in lockstep with the price of cotton that it was common for the price of the former to be determined by multiplying the price of the latter by ten thousand. For example, $0.07 per pound for cotton yielded $700 per slave.[8]

I can't overstate the business impact of slavery. Understanding the money involved will help provide the proper context for the ensuing Civil War. Through 1860, the slave trade accounted for a significant portion of the South's economy. It was estimated that in slave-exporting regions of the antebellum South, the proceeds from the sale of slaves were equivalent in value to 15 percent of the region's staple crop economy.[9] The slaves represented nearly half a billion dollars in property, and they generated wealth for their masters wherever they went.[10]

The capital that funded the slave traders' business had been borrowed from banks, and it had to be repaid with interest. The bodies of the slaves responsible for this economy had to be transported, housed, clothed, fed, and cared for during the one to three months it took to sell them. Some of the slaves were insured in transit; others were covered by life insurance.[11]

Just like any other property, slave sales had to be notarized, and the sellers were taxed. Hundreds of thousands of black people were revenue to the cities and states where they were sold.[12] To that, add the supporting businesses that profited from this trade, including the businesses of landlords, physicians, and insurance agents. It's estimated that the size of this ancillary economy represented 13.5 percent of the price of slaves, which represented tens of millions of dollars over the course of the antebellum period.[13]

The official economic data on slavery that I cite doesn't account for sales between neighbors, state-supervised probate, or debt sales. However, state-supervised and local sales were as much a feature of the antebellum economy as interstate slave trading.[14]

Slavery, however, was becoming less important in the North. There was a growing movement to abolish slavery, which led some northern states to pass laws to abandon slavery. Aside from the fact that slavery was wrong, there was no longer a business reason for slavery in the North, as the North's economy now was based more on industry than agriculture, and they enjoyed a steady stream of European immigrants.[15] In the early 1800s, the poor but rapidly growing rural population in Ireland was largely dependent on producing potatoes. When a fungus struck potato plants across Ireland in the mid-1840s, Irish families sought refuge in the United States.

Before 1830, it's estimated that only five thousand Irish immigrants arrived in the United States per year. With the great potato famine, those numbers skyrocketed to well in excess of half a million.[16] As a result, by 1850, the population of New York City was said to be 26 percent Irish.[17]

Cheap labor is requisite for growth of an industrious nation. With the influx of European immigrants, the North no longer needed slaves to support their growing economy. The Republican Party, newly formed in 1854, became vehemently involved in the issue of slavery, and its members grew more and more vocal regarding their concerns on the matter.

When I think back on the histories of the Republican and Democratic parties and their stances on the black community, I find myself questioning how so many of my fellow black men and women still believe that the Democratic Party has their best interests at heart when history proves they were never on our side. I wonder if they remember that it was the Republican Party that ended slavery. I wonder if they remember that it was the Republican Party that finally recognized us as citizens of our great country. I wonder if they remember that it was the Republican Party that fought for us to finally become members of the American self, while Democrats wanted us to still be classified as the other.

POLITICAL TENSION BETWEEN THE NORTH AND SOUTH

The United States Constitution contained a provision that led to a ban on the importation of African slaves after 1808. It was a business decision. Closing the trade was favorable both to opponents of slavery and to the Virginia slaveholders who feared that the continued importation of slaves would dilute the social power slavery gave them.

The closing of the Atlantic slave trade meant that if southern slave owners wanted to expand their businesses into the newly available western states, they would have to do it with American-born slaves, and they would have to do it by force. However, the North was committed to keeping the western territories open to white labor alone. Slavery added another complexity to an already tense battle over states' rights that had been brewing since the American Revolution.

Members of the young Republican Party strongly opposed the westward expansion of slavery into new states. Northerners became increasingly more polarized against slavery. Harriet Beecher Stowe's book *Uncle Tom's Cabin* made many in the North more aware of slavery's reality. In addition, the Dred Scott case brought the issue of slaves' rights and freedom to the US Supreme Court. Scott, born a slave, moved to a free state with his owner. When his owner died, Scott was denied the chance to purchase his freedom. The US Supreme Court ruled that since he wasn't a citizen, he could not sue in federal court. Nevertheless, his case won over supporters.

By the 1860 presidential election, the young nation was embroiled with problems over slavery, states' rights, and an economy growing stronger in the North. Those issues divided the political parties and reshaped the two-party system.

The Democratic Party was divided between factions in the North and South. The Whig Party—a short-lived effort formed to oppose President Andrew Jackson—had transitioned into the Republican Party, which was largely seen in the North as being in favor of economic advancement.[18] The South, however, saw the Republican Party as a divisive threat.

The 1860 presidential election set the stage for a showdown that would change the course of history. Abraham Lincoln represented the new Republican Party. Stephen Douglas, a northern Democrat, was seen as Lincoln's biggest rival.[19] The Southern Democrats put John C. Breckinridge on the ballot. John C. Bell represented the Constitutional Union Party, a group of former Whigs hoping to avoid secession.[20]

On Election Day, Lincoln won the North, Breckinridge the South, and Bell the border states. Douglas won only Missouri and a part of New Jersey. Lincoln won the popular vote, along with the 180 electoral votes, though none came from the South.

When President Lincoln, a Republican, was elected in 1860, it sealed the deal on the North's stance against the expansion of slavery and on the South's resolve to fight for it. Between Election Day and Lincoln's inauguration in March, seven states seceded from the Union: South Carolina, Mississippi, Florida, Alabama, Georgia, Louisiana, and Texas.[21]

The stage was now set for the seminal political schism that would shape the way forward for the black community in America. Blacks would have two political choices, and initially it would be based simply upon liberty and freedom. That case would be easy to decide, as the Republican Party was established in 1854 really as a one-issue party: restricting the expansion of and ending slavery in America.

It would be a Republican president who would sign the Emancipation Proclamation to free the slaves in the South and allow the first blacks to serve in uniform for this nation in 1863. It would be the Republican Party that would pass and sign into law the Thirteenth, Fourteenth, and Fifteenth Amendments, which would end slavery, make blacks citizens, bestow upon them constitutional rights, and give them the right to vote. The first blacks on Capitol Hill were Republican, and on July 4, 1867—Independence Day—150 blacks were in attendance at the first ever state Republican convention held in Houston, Texas. Just 20 white men attended. By and large, the first Republicans in the state of Texas were black conservatives.[22]

Therefore, from an early political perspective, blacks in America were aligned with the Republican Party, and that was easy to comprehend. The Grand Old Party (GOP) had ended the scourge of slavery in America, as it stood for the liberty and freedom of blacks in America.

Today, the same political schism exists, and it has greatly broadened. It is no longer about physical enslavement but about economic enslavement versus economic emancipation. It is not so much political as it is a matter of principle. However, the schism is still aligned with the existing political parties in America, the same ones who chose different paths in America when it came to slavery.

Today, the choice is as clear as it was for the American black community. Then, our country entered into a brutal Civil War and was divided on the issue of slavery. Today, we are embroiled in a vital ideological war that is centered on whether collective subjugation is the path forward. Then, there were plantations harvesting cotton. Today, we have a twenty-first century economic plantation—our inner cities—controlled by the Democratic Party where the harvest consists of votes.

CHAPTER THREE

BLACK CONSERVATISM AND ITS EARLY CHAMPIONS

When talking about black conservatism, it is important to remind ourselves of the many ways in which black people have embraced the core values that I hold so dear to my heart: a deep sense of honor and respect for family, love and faith in God, an entrepreneurial mind-set to become self-sufficient and financially independent, and the need to pursue an education.

During slavery, it was illegal to teach black men and women how to read and write. Yet around six thousand of them left behind some form of written account that described their lives and struggles. But how could this happen if most of them were illiterate? In some cases, a handful of women—mostly masters' wives, as in the case of Frederick Douglass—took it upon themselves to ignore the law and educate their slaves. Then, educated slaves would pass on their knowledge to fellow slaves and teach them to read and write; some even capitalized on "their skills in literacy as a starting point for leadership careers once slavery ended."[1] Enslaved children, who were at times tasked to carry books for white children going to school, would usually sit outside and listen to the lesson through an open window. In other cases, their stories were told to people they trusted, who then wrote them down on their behalf, as in the case of Venture Smith, whose story was written by Elisha Niles, a schoolteacher.

Born Broteer Furro in West Africa, the son of a prince, he was captured and sold as a slave at the age of six in exchange for "six gallons of rum, and a piece of calico."[2] After being given the name Venture by slave vessel officer Robertson Mumford, "on account of his having purchased me with his own private venture," Smith was taken to Connecticut, where he worked as a slave. He distinguished himself through his self-discipline in saving money to buy freedom not only for himself but also for his wife Meg, also a slave. After his master brutally beat him and stole his money, Smith sought help from a justice of the peace, but with no luck. Eventually, he was sold to merchant Oliver Smith, who gave him the opportunity to work hard to earn enough money to buy his freedom. He worked tirelessly and was finally able to buy not only his own freedom but also his children's and wife's. As a free man, Smith—who had taken his former master's last name as a sign of honor and respect to the man who did not betray him—invested his money in himself and his family. He purchased land and eventually became an entrepreneur, doing a wide variety of jobs, including fishing, farming, and lumbering. His narrative, titled *A Narrative of the Life and Adventures of Venture, a Native of Africa: But Resident above Sixty Years in the United States of America, Related by Himself,* was published in 1798, seven years before his death.

Smith is one example of many other slaves who display the characteristics of conservative values in their respect and love of family, hard work, and shrewd financial and business acumen. However, when talking about black conservatism from slavery to the beginning of the twentieth century, it is not possible to depict a clear picture unless we focus on the pivotal role played by the black church in keeping conservative values alive within the black community. It was mainly within the church that black people were able to secure an education, learn marketable skills, work on their family relationships, and find financial support for their businesses, and it was all centered around the love for God.

Black people's desire to become literate was strong, not only because they could finally read the word of God in the Bible but also because "education was a rebuttal of the prevailing allegation that black people were a different order of human being, incapable of learning and manipulating the master's language."[3] After emancipation, their desire to learn became ever stronger, and freed people of all ages rushed to school to finally gain an education.

In order to meet the needs of the black community, churches quickly transformed themselves into learning centers. For example, "a few of these schools, which were often housed in the basements of black churches, later became famous black colleges. Morehouse College in Atlanta . . . traced its history to a school founded after 1866 in the basement of the Springfield Baptist Church in Augusta. . . . Although it became a predominantly Baptist institution under Booker T. Washington's influence, Tuskegee Institute began as a school which met in the basement of Butler Chapel A.M.E. Zion Church in Tuskegee, Alabama."[4] Although many of the most prominent black universities, such as Howard and Fisk, were also founded by white philanthropists and missionaries, it is important to neither overlook nor underestimate the impact and role played by black churches in supporting the education of the black youth. To this day, black churches independently offer scholarships to their promising youth.

Indeed, the church played a pivotal role in supporting black people in their quest to gain an education, thus becoming the center of the black community, where each member could find solace, support, and strength. It's estimated that black literacy in the South grew from 5 percent in 1870 to 70 percent in 1900.[5]

Black churches also "contributed to the formation of the black self-help tradition and to the establishment of an economic ethos of uplift for the race that emphasized the following virtues and moral values: industry, thrift, discipline, sobriety, and long-term sublimation rather than immediate gratification." Talking to their vast community, "black preachers preached the message of saving for a rainy day, learning to read and write, getting an education, finding a job and working hard, supporting the family, and raising the children respectably and industriously."[6] Even though the economic role of black churches would gain momentum in large part thanks to Booker T. Washington's model of "Negro support for Negro business," it was established and espoused by the black community many years before him.

Clearly, black people have always identified with the core values of conservatism, and since its founding, the Republican Party has always provided blacks with refuge and hope. After all, it was the GOP that freed them from slavery and entrusted them with political leadership positions that would be critical for repairing a divided nation.

As a black Republican, I'm proud that my party involved people with skin like mine from the very beginning. History hasn't always been pretty, but in the Republican Party, a black man found—as Frederick Douglass eloquently put it—"the ark of his safety."[7]

History gifts us a long list of outstanding black men who have embraced the core values of the Republican Party. The names and stories that follow belong to people who have been an inspiration to me, as they represent what it means to be a champion of black conservatism.

ROBERT SMALLS

Perhaps no one embodied the essence of black conservatism and its values as described above more than Robert Smalls. Born a slave in Beaufort, South Carolina, Smalls learned to appreciate the value of the church from his mother, a very religious person. She made sure her son was raised within the black church, thus allowing him to be surrounded and influenced by a community of black leaders. The church environment sparked an interest in Smalls, who sought to socialize with like-minded and like-hearted black people. He found them in the intellectual atmosphere of midcentury Charleston, where he "mingled with free and enslaved blacks at meetings of the seven secret societies he regularly attended, where attendees spoke mostly of welfare measures for blacks, enslaved and free, but also their aspirations to set free the enslaved blacks. With his high native intelligence and gregarious nature, and with the support of his family and owners, Smalls thrived in this intellectual environment."[8]

During the American Civil War, Robert Smalls's independent and entrepreneurial spirit made it possible for him to successfully free himself and his family in an effort so heroic Hollywood couldn't make it up. It was common for the Confederate Army to use black slaves as soldiers in their fight against Union forces. Smalls was assigned to steer the CSS *Planter*, a lightly armed Confederate military transport ship, with the purpose of delivering dispatches, troops, and supplies to survey waterways and to lay mines. Smalls regularly piloted the *Planter* throughout Charleston harbor and beyond, on rivers in the area and along the South Carolina, Georgia, and Florida coasts.[9]

On May 12, 1862, the *Planter* traveled ten miles southwest of Charleston to stop at Coles Island, a Confederate post on the Stono River that was being dismantled.[10] There the ship picked up guns to transport to a fort in Charleston harbor. At some point, Smalls's family members had hid aboard another steamer docked at North Atlantic Wharf.[11]

On the evening of May 12, the *Planter* was docked as usual at the wharf below General Ripley's headquarters.[12] Three white officers disembarked to spend the night ashore, leaving Smalls and the crew on board, "as was their custom." Afterward, the three Confederate officers were court-martialed and two convicted, but the verdicts were later overturned.[13]

Around 3:00 a.m. on May 13, Smalls and seven of the eight slave crewmen made their previously planned escape to the Union blockade ships. Smalls put on the captain's uniform and wore a straw hat similar to the captain's. He sailed the *Planter* past what was then called Southern Wharf and stopped at another wharf to pick up his wife, his children, and the families of other crewmen.[14]

Smalls guided the ship past the five Confederate harbor forts without incident, as he gave the correct signals at checkpoints. The *Planter* had been commanded by a Captain Charles C. J. Relyea, and Smalls copied Relyea's manners and straw hat on deck to fool Confederate onlookers on the shore and in the forts. The *Planter* sailed past Fort Sumter at about 4:30 a.m. The alarm was only raised by the time they were out of gun range. Smalls headed straight for the Union Navy fleet, replacing the rebel flags with a white bedsheet his wife had brought aboard. The *Planter* had been seen by the USS *Onward*, which was about to fire until a crewman spotted the white flag. In the dark, the sheet was hard to see, but the sunrise came just in time.[15]

A witness recounted:

> Just as No. 3 port gun was being elevated, someone cried out, "I see something that looks like a white flag"; and true enough there was something flying on the steamer that would have been white by application of soap and water. As she neared us, we looked in vain for the face of a white man. When they discovered that we would not fire on them, there was a rush of contrabands out on her deck, some dancing, some singing, whistling, jumping; and others stood looking towards Fort Sumter, and muttering all sorts of maledictions against it, and 'de heart of de Souf,' generally. As the steamer came near, and under the stern of the Onward, one of the Colored men stepped forward, and taking off his hat, shouted, "Good morning, sir! I've brought you some of the old United States guns, sir!" That man was Robert Smalls.[16]

After the Civil War, Smalls returned to South Carolina and truly became the personification of black conservatism by devoting "himself and his resources unstintingly to the principal objectives of acquiring an adequate home for his growing family, establishing economic viability for them through entrepreneurship, helping to sustain independent black churches, and launching a series of events to bring education to himself, his family, and the other children in the community."[17]

Once black men were finally granted the right to vote, he became a politician, winning an election as a Republican to the South Carolina State Legislature and the United States House of Representatives during the Reconstruction era.

HIRAM REVELS

A freeman his entire life, Hiram Rhodes Revels was the first African American to serve in the US Congress. With his moderate political orientation and oratorical skills honed from years as a preacher, Revels filled a vacant seat in the United States Senate in 1870. Just before the Senate agreed to admit a black man to its ranks on February 25, Republican senator Charles Sumner of Massachusetts sized up the importance of the moment: "All men are created equal, says the great Declaration," Sumner roared, "and now a great act attests this verity. Today we make the Declaration a reality . . . The Declaration was only half established by Independence. The greatest duty remained behind. In assuring the equal rights of all we complete the work."[18]

Hiram Rhodes Revels was born to free parents in Fayetteville, North Carolina, on September 27, 1827. His father worked as a Baptist preacher, and his mother was of Scottish descent. Revels was raised surrounded by principles of black conservatism—a sense of belonging within the black church community, an entrepreneurial mind-set, advocacy for the importance of education, strong family values—and the virtues of his upbringing were mirrored in his many accomplishments. As a young man, he received his education "at a school run by a free black woman. Perhaps her influences as a Southern black educator helped to shape

29

his lifelong interest and commitment to teaching and promoting the educational affairs of Afro-Americans."[19]

Revels took on many different jobs—including barber and teacher—before moving north to complete his education in 1844. He attended the Beech Grove Quaker Seminary in Liberty, Indiana, and the Darke County Seminary for black students in Ohio. In 1845, Revels was ordained in the African Methodist Episcopal (AME) Church.

Revels traveled throughout the country, carrying out religious work and educating blacks in Indiana, Illinois, Kansas, Kentucky, and Tennessee.[20] Although Missouri forbade free blacks to live in the state for fear they would instigate uprisings, Revels took a pastorate at an AME church in St. Louis in 1853, noting that the law was "seldom enforced." However, Revels later revealed he had to be careful because of restrictions on his movements. "I sedulously refrained from doing anything that would incite slaves to run away from their masters," he recalled. "It being understood that my object was to preach the gospel to them, and improve their moral and spiritual condition even slave holders were tolerant of me."[21] Despite his cautiousness, Revels was imprisoned for preaching to the black community in 1854. Upon his release, he accepted a position with the Presbyterian Church in Baltimore, Maryland, working alongside his brother, Willis Revels, also an AME pastor. Hiram Revels was the principal of a black school in Baltimore and subsequently attended Knox College in Galesburg, Illinois, on a scholarship from 1855 to 1857.

When the Civil War broke out in 1861, Revels helped recruit two black regiments from Maryland. In 1862, when black soldiers were permitted to fight, he served as the chaplain for a black regiment in campaigns in Vicksburg and Jackson, Mississippi. In 1863, Revels returned to St. Louis, where he established a freedmen's school. At the end of hostilities, Revels served in a church in Leavenworth, Kansas.[22]

Before the Civil War, fewer than a thousand free black Mississippians had access to a basic education. Thus, leadership from freedmen such as Revels became vital to the Republican Party for rallying the new electorate in the postwar years.[23] It was through his work in education that Revels became involved in politics, taking his first elected position as a Natchez alderman in 1868. He entered politics reluctantly, fearing racial friction and interference with his religious work, but he quickly won over blacks and whites with his moderate and compassionate political opinions.

In 1869, Revels won a seat in the Mississippi State Senate. Under the newly installed Reconstruction government, Revels was one of more than thirty blacks among the state's 140 legislators. Upon his election, he wrote a friend in Leavenworth, Kansas: "We are in the midst of an exciting canvass . . . I am working very hard in politics as well as in other matters. We are determined that Mississippi shall be settled on a basis of justice and political and legal equality."[24]

The primary task of the newly elected state senate was to fill US Senate seats. In 1861, Democrat Albert Brown and future Confederate president Jefferson Davis had both vacated Mississippi's US Senate seats when the state seceded from the Union. When their terms expired in 1865 and 1863 respectively, their seats were not filled and remained vacant.

In 1870, the new Mississippi state legislature wished to elect a black man to fill the remainder of one term—due to expire in 1871 for the seat once held by Brown—but was determined to fill the other unexpired term, ending in 1875, with a white candidate. Black legislators agreed to the deal, believing, as Revels recalled, that an election of one of their own would "be a weakening blow against color line prejudice." The Democratic minority also endorsed the plan, hoping a black senator would "seriously damage the Republican Party."[25]

After three days and seven ballots, on January 20, 1870, the Mississippi state legislature voted eighty-five to fifteen to seat Hiram

Revels in Brown's former seat. They chose Union general Adelbert Ames to fill Davis's former seat.[26]

Revels arrived in Washington at the end of January 1870 but could not present his credentials until Mississippi was readmitted to the United States on February 23. Senate Republicans sought to swear in Revels immediately afterward, but Senate Democrats were determined to block the effort. Led by senators Garrett Davis of Kentucky and Willard Saulsbury of Delaware, the Democrats claimed Revels's election was null and void, arguing that Mississippi was under military rule and lacked a civil government to confirm his election. Others claimed Revels had not been a US citizen until the passage of the Fourteenth Amendment in 1868 and was therefore ineligible to become a US senator. Senate Republicans rallied to his defense. Though Revels would not fill Davis's seat, the symbolism of a black man's admission to the Senate after the departure of the former president of the Confederacy was not lost on Radical Republicans. Nevada senator James Nye underlined the significance of this event:

> [Jefferson Davis] went out to establish a government whose cornerstone should be the oppression and perpetual enslavement of a race because their skin differed in color from his," Nye declared. "Sir, what a magnificent spectacle of retributive justice is witnessed here today! In the place of that proud, defiant man, who marched out to trample underfoot the Constitution and the laws of the country he had sworn to support, comes back one of that humble race whom he would have enslaved forever to take and occupy his seat upon this floor.
>
> On the afternoon of February 25, the Senate voted 48 to 8 to seat Revels, who subsequently received assignments to the Committee on Education and Labor and the Committee on the District of Columbia.[27]

FREDERICK DOUGLASS

If black conservatism means being a self-starter and an independent human being who does not rely on handouts, has strong family values, loves the black community, and fears God, then Frederick Douglass is black conservatism in the flesh. An advocate for black communal self-help, individualism, and men's right to bear arms, Douglass was also an avid supporter of education as the only way for enslaved men and women to finally gain freedom and have the opportunity to advance in society.

In his own autobiography, titled *Narrative of the Life of Frederick Douglass: An American Slave*, he recounts the moment when his master, Mr. Auld, found out that his wife, Mrs. Auld, had been secretly teaching young Douglass to read and write:

> "If you teach that nigger (speaking of myself) how to read, there would be no keeping him. It would forever unfit him to be a slave. He would at once become unmanageable and of no value to his master. As to himself, it could do him no good, but a great deal of harm. It would make him discontented and unhappy." These words sank deep into my heart, stirred up sentiments within that lay slumbering, and called into existence an entirely new train of thought. . . . From that moment, I understood the pathway from slavery to freedom. . . . Whilst I was saddened by the thought of losing the aid of my kind mistress, I was gladdened by the invaluable instruction which . . . I had gained from my master. Though conscious of the difficulty of learning without a teacher, I set out with high hope, and a fixed purpose, at whatever cost of trouble, to learn how to read.[28]

Perhaps the most well known of the first black Republicans, Douglass escaped from slavery and became a national leader of the abolitionist movement in Massachusetts and New York. His intelligent way of communicating muted the arguments of slaveholders who claimed that slaves lacked the capacity to function as independent American citizens. Douglass was an author of several books and a gifted orator who bravely spoke in favor of women's suffrage when even white men were silent to support them.

When you read arguments from Douglass where he urges blacks to join the Republican Party, you'll find that they still hold up today. He was baffled at how some blacks would still want to side with the Democratic Party that enslaved them.

In the 1883 letter below, Douglass expresses his loyalty to the Republican Party. He had just appeared at the National Convention of Colored Men in Louisville, where he gave a speech urging black men to stand up for their rights.[29] Only a week after this letter appeared, the US Supreme Court stuck down the Civil Rights Act of 1875, paving the way for Jim Crow laws that segregated the South for another century.

In response to a question from a Private Dalzell about his attitude on race, Douglass wrote:

Washington DC, Oct. 3—My Dear Dalzell: Your letter came to me in the midst of the Louisville convention. I had no time to acknowledge and thank you for it at the moment, as I should have gladly done. I have read it, and can bear witness to the truth that you have ever been a true friend of my people and of the Republican Party. I concede to you the gift of prophecy, and should like to have you tell me whom the Republican Party will put in nomination next year. I see that my views at the Louisville convention are variously commented upon.

I am thought to be an Independent, and so I am, but I am an Independent inside of the Republican Party. I can have all the independence I want inside of the Republican Party. I am both independent and dependent. I do not take a step in life that I am not dependent on somebody or something. In politics I am dependent upon one or the other political party, and I am foolish enough to think that the Republican Party may as safely be trusted with the destiny of the Republic and the rights of the colored people as the Democratic Party, and in this I know I am right.

For the life of me I cannot see how any honest colored man who has brains enough to put two ideas together can allow himself under the notion of independence to give aid and comfort to the Democratic Party in Ohio or elsewhere. Woe to the colored people of this country when the Republican Party shall triumph in spite of the treacherous votes of colored men. Bad as our condition now is, it would be worse then. We should neither have nor deserve the confidence of any party, and would, to use a slang phrase, "Be out in the cold." My advice to colored men everywhere is to stick to the Republican Party. Tell your wants, hold the party up to its profession, but do your utmost to keep it in power in State and Nation.

What I said at Louisville about the election of a colored man to the Vice-Presidency has been perverted. What I said was that no class of American people could afford to be excluded from participation in the administration of the Government, and when a colored man could be elected to the Vice-Presidency or hold a seat in the Cabinet, the color line would no longer be significant.

My views on this subject are given in the last paragraph of my address, which I send you herewith: "We hold it to be self-evident that no class or color should be the exclusive rulers of the country. If there is such a ruling class there must of course be a subject class, and when this condition is once established this government by the people, of the people, and for the people will have already perished from the earth."

I hope you will allow no man to tell you uncontradicted that I am not now, as I ever have been, a firm and inflexible Republican. The convention at Louisville was non-partisan. The objects sought were broader than party and appealed to the justice of the American people at large. My hands are full of work, as doubtless yours are, and I will not write further now.

Your friend,
Frederick Douglass[30]

NORRIS WRIGHT CUNEY

Maud Cuney Hare, Norris Wright Cuney's daughter, communicates a selfless and caring image of her father in her book *Norris Writght Cuney: A Tribune of the Black People*. Described as a man with solid conservative values who believed in the right to bear arms and worked hard to improve the quality of black people's lives—he suffered from insomnia, so he used the extra hours to work even harder—and a family man who taught his children to "do as you please, but please to do right,"[31] Cuney was a self-starter who educated himself on literature and law, with Shakespeare being his all-time favorite poet.

His determination to help the black community eventually led him to become the highest-ranking Republican in the state of Texas. His ability to simultaneously generate opportunities for black entrepreneurs and win over the trust of white politicians was unparalleled. The fourth of eight children, Cuney was born on May 12, 1846, to a white planter and a slave mother near Hempstead, Texas. He attended George B. Vahon's Wylie Street School for blacks in Pittsburgh, Pennsylvania, from 1859 to the beginning of the Civil War.[32]

After a period of wandering around on riverboats and working odd jobs, he returned to Texas and settled in Galveston. There he studied law, and by July 18, 1871, he was appointed president of the Galveston Union League.[33]

In 1873 Cuney was appointed secretary of the Republican State Executive Committee. Though he ran for mayor of Galveston in 1875 and for the state House and Senate in 1876 and 1882, he was defeated in all races. What I admire about Cuney is he didn't let those defeats define him.

He used his power in appointed positions to help others. He went on to serve as a delegate to every Republican National Convention from 1872 to 1892.[34]

In 1873 he presided at the state convention of black leaders, which was held in Texas on at least ten occasions during the period from Reconstruction through the 1890s to express the concerns of blacks.[35] To me, it's impressive how these black men, just a few years removed from slavery, were brave and organized enough to start pushing for civil rights. It's an image of black conservatism—in Texas, no less—of which many are unaware. In a meeting of the Texas State Central Committee of Colored Men on March 22, 1866, the group opposed a request for funds for former slaves because their members did not trust the man asking for the money.[36] Instead, the committee members opted to send resources to the Freedmen's Bureau.

Cuney lead the group during the convention on July 4, 1873, when the topics on the agenda were friendly race relations, a federal civil rights act, open political meetings, black landholding, internal improvements, immigration to the United States, President Ulysses S. Grant, and the Republican Party.[37] What an honor it would have been to be in that room among these distinguished delegates, making historic leadership decisions as the country was healing from the Civil War.

Cuney then became inspector of customs of the port of Galveston and revenue inspector at Sabine Pass in 1872, special inspector of customs at Galveston in 1882, and finally collector of customs of the port of Galveston in 1889.[38] It's one thing to have the trust of your own people as a leader, but for Cuney to get white political leaders in a city as big as Galveston to trust him with money speaks volumes about his character and power of influence. Keep in mind that during this period, the city of Galveston was a major port city and had more notoriety than Dallas—arguably more than Austin.

In 1883, Cuney was an alderman from the twelfth district on the Galveston City Council, which afforded him time to still serve as leader of the Republican Party in Texas. In 1886, he became Texas's national committeeman of the Republican Party, which made him unofficially the most important black political figure in the South during the nineteenth century.[39] He was so influential in Texas that one historian referred to the period between 1884 and 1896 as the "Cuney Era."

He was able to lead whites and blacks, fighting diligently for the rights of black dockworkers in Galveston and for education for blacks as an early supporter of what is now Prairie View A&M University. Cuney died on March 3, 1898, in San Antonio and was buried in Lake View Cemetery of Galveston.[40]

JOSIAH T. WALLS

In 2010, I became the first black Republican to represent Florida in Congress since Rep. Josiah Thomas Walls, who served during Reconstruction. Therefore, this esteemed lineup of black leaders who first embraced the principles of black conservatism—allowing me, many years later, to write my American black conservative manifesto—would not be complete without him.

"He's not running for office just for him," University of Florida history lecturer Steven Noll said about Walls. "He's running for office for his race." Indeed, Walls's main focus was on how to help the black community advance and finally gain what was rightfully theirs. An avid supporter of black-owned businesses, black newspapers, and black education, he represented the definition of a self-made man with an entrepreneurial mind. He owned a "large orange grove just outside of Gainesville and would ship his oranges into the city by boat through what is now Paynes Prairie Preserve State Park. A man born a slave now had his own plantation."[41]

Walls was born into slavery in Winchester, Virginia, on December 30, 1842. When the Civil War started, he was forced to be a private servant to a Confederate artilleryman until he was captured by Union soldiers in May 1862.[42]

After being emancipated by his Union captors, Walls attended school in Harrisburg, Pennsylvania. By July 1863, he was serving in the Union Army as part of the Third Infantry Regiment of the United States Colored Troops.[43]

He moved to Florida with his Union troop and spent the remainder of his life there. During Reconstruction, Walls was one of few educated black men in Florida. Like a handful of other educated black men during this transformational period, Walls suddenly had options regarding what he could do with his life.

He started his political career representing north-central Florida's Alachua County in the 1868 Florida constitutional convention. That same year, he ran a successful campaign for state assemblyman. Then, in 1869, he was elected to the state senate as one of five freedmen in the twenty-four-man chamber.[44]

I'm proud of Walls because he ran for office at a time when well-organized Jacksonville branches of the Ku Klux Klan were intimidating Florida's freedmen into avoiding the polls on Election Day.

In the 1870 nominating convention, senior Republican leaders wanted to nominate a black man to the state's sole at-large seat in the

US House of Representatives to renew black voters' courage and faith in the Republican Party. In looking at their options, Walls stood out because of his reputation as an independent politician.[45]

In the general election for that seat, Walls ran against former slave owner and Confederate veteran Silas L. Niblack, who attacked Walls's capabilities. Niblack argued that a former slave was not educated enough to serve in Congress. Not shy of a challenge, Walls agreed to debate Niblack and spoke against him at several political rallies. The campaign turned so violent that a would-be assassin's bullet narrowly missed Walls by just a few inches at a Gainesville rally.[46]

Walls won the election over Niblack by 627 votes out of more than 24,000 votes cast. He was sworn in to the Forty-Second Congress of 1871. However, Niblack contested the election, saying that canvassers illegally rejected Democratic ballots. For his part, Walls claimed that the Ku Klux Klan was also working against his own election, but he still won.[47]

In a rare decision, two years after Walls was in office, the Republican majority opted to back Niblack and declared him the winner. Walls was eventually appointed to other positions and won future elections, including one in 1876 to be a Florida state senator.

While our terms were separated by time, I was humbled to carry on his legacy with my election to the House in November 2010. I have since committed myself to ensuring that Walls's legacy, and others like his, remain intact by inspiring others and reminding my fellow black men and women of the core values of the Republican Party.

CHAPTER FOUR

GAINS LOST AND THE RISE OF JIM CROW LAWS

It's hard to find another period in the political history of the United States of America that better highlights the differences in core values between the Republican Party and the Democratic Party than the era of Jim Crow laws. The name Jim Crow derives from "Jump Jim Crow," a song and dance show performed by white actor Thomas Rice, who would use blackface to denigrate and convey an insulting caricature of a disabled African slave. Many state statutes were passed to legalize racial segregation and dictate when, where, and how black people could live, thus formally—and legally—placing them in a state of forced servitude.

During this period, which lasted roughly a hundred years (from 1865 until 1968), the Democratic Party went above and beyond to make sure that black people could no longer benefit from the freedom and rights they were finally able to enjoy thanks to the Republican Party.

It all began after the Civil War, when Congress tried to keep southerners from reestablishing white supremacy by deploying the US Army to rule over most of the South. Those states were not allowed back into the Union until they ratified the Fourteenth Amendment, which prohibited states from denying "the equal protection of the laws" to all US citizens, including their newly freed slaves.

After states were readmitted back into the Union they sought to regain control through a myriad of discriminatory restrictions known as Jim Crow laws. Southern states used them to get around the Fifteenth Amendment, ratified in 1870, which stated: "The right of citizens of the United States to vote shall not be denied or abridged by the United

States or by any State on account of race, color, or previous condition of servitude."

For decades, the southern states worked to keep more than half a million black men from casting their ballots for the Republican Party—the party that ended their slavery.

Take Mississippi, for example. When Mississippi rejoined the Union in 1870, former slaves made up more than half of the state's population.[1] There was no way a Democrat would win an election. In the following years, Mississippi elected blacks such as Hiram Revels to Congress and also elected a number of other black state officials, including a lieutenant governor.[2]

For the first time, blacks had a shot at freedom. They were still largely poor, but they had rights and protections under the law like other citizens. That all changed in 1877 when the Reconstruction period ended.

When federal troops left Mississippi, blacks no longer had protections, and the white supremacy of the Democrats took over. As a result, black voting fell off sharply because of threats by white employers and violence from the Ku Klux Klan.[3]

Whites began voting out the Republicans and replaced them with Democratic governors, legislators, and local officials. To keep blacks under control, they issued laws dictating that many things were to be banned—such as interracial marriages—and that public places, such as railroad cars and schools, had to be racially segregated.

In 1890, Mississippi held a convention to write a new state constitution to replace the one forced on them since Reconstruction. The white leaders of the convention were clear about their intentions. "We came here to exclude the Negro," declared the convention president.[4] Because of the Fifteenth Amendment, they could not ban blacks from voting. Instead, they wrote into the state constitution a number of restrictions that made it difficult for most blacks to register to vote.

Among the restrictions, Mississippi required an annual poll tax, which voters had to pay for two years before the election. Blacks also had to pass a literacy test, requiring the voter to read a section of the state constitution and then explain it to the county clerk who processed voter registrations.[5] The clerk, who was white, determined whether the voter was literate enough. Then there was the infamous "grandfather clause," which allowed registration for anyone whose grandfather voted before the Civil War.

Mississippi cut the percentage of black men registered to vote from more than 90 percent during Reconstruction to less than 6 percent by 1892, according to research from the Constitutional Rights Foundation. Mississippi's measures were copied by most of the other southern states during this period.

In his 1903 essay "The Disfranchisement of the Negro," Charles W. Chesnutt puts the case for blacks to the American people very plainly. Chesnutt, one of the nation's first widely recognized black novelists, begins his argument by taking on the Jim Crow laws that were preventing blacks in the South from voting.

"[Voting] is plainly declared and firmly fixed by the Constitution. No such person is called upon to present reasons why he should possess this right: that question is foreclosed by the Constitution," Chesnutt said. "The object of the elective franchise is to give representation. So long as the Constitution retains its present form, any State Constitution, or statute, which seeks, by juggling the ballot, to deny the colored race fair representation, is a clear violation of the fundamental law of the land."

Chesnutt argued that during the thirty-five years of the Fifteenth Amendment, blacks had made rapid strides in education, wealth, character, and self-respect. "A generation has grown to manhood and womanhood under the great, inspiring freedom conferred by the Constitution and protected by the right of suffrage—protected in large degree by the mere naked right, even when its exercise was hindered or denied by unlawful means," he said.

The effectiveness of Jim Crow laws in excluding the black vote is seen clearly in Alabama's registration statistics. According to the census of 1900, of a total 181,471 Negro "males of voting age," fewer than 3,000 were registered; in Montgomery County alone, the seat of the state capital, where there were 7,000 Negro males of voting age, only 47 were allowed to register, while in several counties not one single Negro was permitted to vote.[6]

Where the black man had a friend in the US Congress to pass laws, he had an enemy in the US Supreme Court, which supported Jim Crow laws, thus keeping him from advancing.

Voter discrimination cases were brought before the Supreme Court. However, the court held that since there was no ambiguity in the language used and the "Negro" was not directly named, the Court would not go behind the wording of the Constitution to find a meaning that discriminated against the colored voter.[7]

In the case of *Jackson v. Giles*, brought by a black citizen of Montgomery, Alabama, the Supreme Court confesses itself impotent to provide a remedy for what, by inference, it acknowledges may be a "great political wrong"—careful to avoid, however, stating that it is a wrong.[8]

"The colored people are left, in the states where they have been disfranchised, absolutely without representation, direct or indirect, in any law-making body, in any court of justice, in any branch of government—for the feeble remnant of voters left by law is so inconsiderable as to be without a shadow of power," Chesnutt wrote.

It should be clear by now that Democrats were the party of black suppression. Today they are the party of black regression, which will be clear in the later chapters as we look at how Democrats gradually started offering blacks freebies so they could use them as pawns to gain political leverage in Washington.

Given their history, you somewhat expect that behavior from racist whites. What's incomprehensible to me are the blacks who mindlessly follow along—hook, line, and sinker.

Yes, times have changed. Blacks in the 1950s created a civil rights movement. They launched voter registration drives in many southern communities. They experienced a lot of pain, including denial of voting rights and the murder of Medgar Evers, a civil rights movement activist, World War II veteran, and father of three who was killed in 1963 at the age of thirty-seven by Klansman and white supremacist Byron De La Beckwith, who was finally found guilty of the murder and sentenced to life in prison in 1994. But we now have equal protections under the law.

The responsibility now shifts to blacks today to do their part and to remember the hard road that was paved for them. We finally have been guaranteed equality of opportunity; demands for equality of outcomes were never part of the plan for early black leaders.

To this end, I leave you with parting words from Chesnutt:

> Finally, there is, somewhere in the Universe a 'Power that works for righteousness,' and that leads men to do justice to one another. To this power, working upon the hearts and consciences of men, the Negro can always appeal. He has the right upon his side, and in the end the right will prevail. The Negro will, in time, attain to full manhood and citizenship throughout the United States. No better guaranty of this is needed than a comparison of his present with his past. Toward this he must do his part, as lies within his power and his opportunity.[9]

CHAPTER FIVE

THE FATHER OF BLACK CONSERVATISM: BOOKER T. WASHINGTON

One black man whose voice spoke louder than others' during the era of Jim Crow laws was the man I find most inspiring and look up to as my mentor: Booker T. Washington. Yes, Chesnutt challenged the black man "to do his part, as lies within his power and his opportunity," but his contemporary Booker T. Washington laid the blueprint for how that should be done.[1]

At a time when blacks were looking for leadership in the midst of stifling Jim Crow laws, Washington stepped forward with a practical plan for success that wasn't as dependent on the whims of whites. Though there were blacks practicing conservative principles even before him, Washington's ability to clearly articulate the call to action for blacks—especially in the era in which he did it—set him apart as the father of black conservatism.

Washington was born a slave on a farm in Virginia in 1856. Slavery ended when he was nine years old, but his work in a salt furnace and as a houseboy for a white family continued. Growing up during the Reconstruction period, Washington had a front-row seat to the seismic changes taking place in the country.

He went to school at Hampton Institute, recognized as one of the earliest freedmen's schools specializing in industrial education. In 1881, Washington would build his own school in Alabama, the Tuskegee Institute, to focus on industrial education as well:

> Many seem to think that industrial education is meant to make the Negro work as he worked in the days of slavery. This is far

from my conception of industrial education. If this training is worth anything to the Negro, it consists in teaching him how not to work, but how to make the forces of nature—air, steam, water, horsepower, and electricity—work for him. If it has any value it is in lifting labor up out of toil and drudgery into the plane of the dignified and the beautiful. The Negro in the South works and works hard; but too often his ignorance and lack of skill causes him to do his work in the most costly and shiftless manner, and this keeps him near the bottom of the ladder in the economic world.[2]

At the Tuskegee Institute, Washington practiced what he preached. In 1903, the school owned two thousand acres, of which eight hundred were cultivated each year by the students of the school. At the school, students learned blacksmithing, carpentry, printing, harness making, shoemaking, brick masonry and brick making, sawmilling, mechanical and architectural drawing, electrical and steam engineering, agriculture, stock raising, horticulture, tailoring, laundry work, cooking, sewing, and housekeeping.

For Washington, it was important that blacks in this new postslavery environment learn the difference between being worked and working. Being worked meant degradation, while working meant civilization. He preached that all forms of labor were honorable and all forms of idleness disgraceful.

True "higher education," according to Washington, involved teaching the generation of his day what it meant to work and save. "All races that have got upon their feet have done so largely by laying an economic foundation, and, in general, by beginning in a proper cultivation and ownership of the soil."[3]

I'm often asked why I uplift Washington's name so much in speeches. I do so because I want to remind people that there is a better way of living. His streamlined message of hard work and maintaining gritty self-reliance speaks volumes even today—to all people, especially blacks.

By nearly every statistical measurement today, we're lagging far behind the economic curve. If, in his day, Washington wouldn't allow fellow blacks to use even a former life of slavery and their current Jim Crow laws as an excuse, then imagine how he would react today to black America waiting on progressive socialists to give them gifts regardless of work.

On these plantations, black men and women were constantly being trained not only as farmers but as carpenters, blacksmiths, wheelwrights, brick masons, engineers, cooks, seamstresses, and housekeepers. Though this industrial training on plantations was crude and given for selfish purposes, it left blacks at the close of the war in possession of nearly all the common and skilled labor in the South.

Washington argued that blacks should seize the moment as a strategic opportunity. The industries that gave the South its power were now essentially under the control of a free black population.

Yet he faced opposition in that line of thinking. Scholars like W. E. B. Du Bois argued that it was time for blacks to lay aside the plow and demand leadership positions at the highest levels of government. Du Bois wanted blacks to pursue a more holistic education. "Men we shall have only as we make manhood the object of the work of the schools—intelligence, broad sympathy, knowledge of the world that was and is, and of the relation of men to it—this is the curriculum of that Higher Education which must underlie true life," Du Bois said in his own 1903 essay, entitled "The Talented Tenth."[4]

The words of Frederick Douglass, who by then had already died, rang immortal in summarizing why Washington's ideology had to take preeminence before Du Bois's ideology could even be considered. "Every blow of the sledge hammer wielded by a sable arm is a powerful blow in support of our cause. Every colored mechanic is by virtue of circumstances an elevator of his race. Every house built by a black man is a strong tower against the allied hosts of prejudice. It is impossible for us to attach too much importance to this aspect of the subject. Without industrial development there can be no wealth; without wealth there can be no leisure; without leisure no opportunity for thoughtful reflection and the cultivation of the higher arts," Douglass said.[5]

Washington, continuing his defense against contemporaries like Du Bois, said: "I would set no limits to the attainments of the Negro in arts, in letters or statesmanship, but I believe the surest way to reach those ends is by laying the foundation in the little things of life that lie immediately about one's door. I plead for industrial education and development for the Negro not because I want to cramp him, but because I want to free him. I want to see him enter the all-powerful business and commercial world."[6]

One early entrepreneur who followed Washington's example was Madam C. J. Walker, one of the first black female millionaires in America. The first child born into freedom in her family, C. J. Walker struggled through decades in the cotton fields and as a poorly paid laundress before her ingenuity and her determination to give her child an education led her to reach out for what was right in front of her door and step into a world of entrepreneurship. The sister of four brothers who worked as barbers, Walker, who suffered from a scalp condition, employed her God-given talents to not only solve her ailment but make a fortune doing so. She developed her own line of hair-care products and, through good, old-fashioned hard work, became a national name in what she called "the greatest country under the sun."[7] As part of her business model, C. J. Walker offered education and advancement opportunities to other black women, establishing Lelia College to train beauty culturists to their work. She was diligent about giving to black American causes—including the Tuskegee Institute of Booker T. Washington, who became a friend of hers—until the day she died.

Looking at our current state of affairs, we could all stand to benefit from the example of innovators like Madam C. J. Walker and Booker T. Washington. We still need Washington's tutelage. I'm concerned that, in too many of our urban cities, we're headed down a dangerous path of progressive socialism. A path on which young people grow up with a sense of entitlement; a path on which kids are saddling themselves with college debt by majoring in subjects with questionable benefits to society; a path on which industrial and vocational training is looked down upon.

The challenge for blacks today is to make Washington's message relevant to the current world. We need to think strategically about the skill sets that are in high demand and have a high trajectory of growth. Right now, science, technology, engineering, and math should be at the top of the list.

Washington is a personal hero of mine; he valued education in the same way my own parents valued it, as they sacrificed to put me in a tough Catholic school in inner-city Atlanta when I was a boy. I learned hard lessons—intellectual, practical, and moral—that laid the foundation for my own success in life.

As Washington himself said, "The world cares very little what you or I know, but it does care a great deal about what you or I do." I found that to be the case as I advanced first in the military world and then in civilian life.

Today, we must spend our time ensuring that families throughout America, no matter their zip code, can rely upon the twin pillars that Washington cited as the foundations of prosperity: education and entrepreneurship.

That means real choice in education, with power restored to parents, who will always make better decisions on their children's behalf than bureaucrats. It means advocating entrepreneurship by rolling back onerous regulations that prevent Americans from pursuing their dreams.

Washington believed in his students. He had faith that with the right education and opportunities, they could remake the world. If he could have that type of resolve even given the challenges of his day, what's our excuse?

Why do I refer to Washington as the father of black conservatism? The answer is simple. He espoused the most fundamental conservative principle: individual entrepreneurial spirit. He realized that, as my folks taught me, education is the great equalizer that unlocks the doors of opportunity. No free man or woman should leave their life up to someone else to determine the outcome. And if this former slave could rise to become one of the great orators and educators in America—a man who hosted an American president at Tuskegee Normal and Industrial Institute and dined with another in the White House—then what excuse do we have in the black community today?

We need to stop the incessant, depressing pity party about being held down and held back. Every person in America should read Washington's autobiography *Up from Slavery* and ask: Did Washington ask for reparations? Did he await a welfare check from da gubmint? Did he run about protesting, decrying, and demanding social justice? No; he was a true man of conservative principles who realized that freedom is empowering and that the greatest form of empowerment is economic empowerment, not economic enslavement.

CHAPTER SIX

"TO SUPPORT AND DEFEND . . ."

In today's fractured society, many young black men and women look up to athletes, rappers, singers, and other entertainers who have no problem publicly and loudly disrespecting the American flag and anthem and what they stand for. Social media has made it too easy for this generation to follow their favorite celebrities, who mostly preach sinful values—promiscuity and misogyny, for example—and flaunt their material possessions, such as expensive cars, big mansions, flashy jewelry, and so on.

As a result, young black men and women believe that, in order to be "somebody" in this world, you have to live that type of lifestyle. But what about their core values as black people? What about the importance of family, the drive to succeed academically or in the workplace, and the honor of putting on the American military uniform and protecting our country? Is this generation even aware of the outstanding black people who succeeded against the most unspeakable violence and disrespect so that their great-grandchildren could finally have their freedom and rights recognized and respected?

I believe it's time we remind them of the real black heroes—the ones who proudly wore that uniform to defend our country's freedom even when they were not free themselves. It's time to remind them that real black heroes don't disrespect the flag. They don't disrespect their families. They don't disrespect the military. On the contrary, they live each day by following the core values our flag represents, working hard to provide for their families, and serving their country with honor.

Along with Booker T. Washington, Frederick Douglass and Corporal Herman West Sr. were two other black men who have had a profound impact on my life. Frederick Douglass, who was born a slave but then became the most stentorian voice for abolition and the end of slavery, highlighted the importance of serving our country when he said, "Once let the black man get upon his person the brass letter, US, let him get an eagle on his button, and a musket on his shoulder and bullets in his pocket, there is no power on earth that can deny that he has earned the right to citizenship."[1]

Corporal Herman West Sr., who to my eyes is the embodiment of Frederick Douglass's dream, once told me, "Boy, there is no greater honor than to wear the uniform of the United States of America. I want you to be the first officer in our family."

The connection of those two quotes has not had an impact only upon me. Since Douglass spoke those immortal words, countless black men and women have worn those brass letters—US—upon their chests.

Black conservatism is not anything new, but its principles have been forgotten. There has been a lapse in subsequent generations honoring the sage wisdom of our forefathers and foremothers, who, through immense adversity, evidenced the resilience, perseverance, and character that demands our regard.

The values reflected in the history of the black community are faith, family, individual responsibility, excellence through quality education, and service to the nation. It does not take any highly intellectual analysis—especially for someone like me, the third of four generations of combat veterans in the family—to see that somewhere along the way, we stopped teaching the history that did not accommodate a certain narrative. We make movies, but we have stopped telling the stories of the men and women who were American heroes in the black community. We have allowed the voices of radicalism to take the position of denigrating service to the United States of America. How was it possible for a man born in the South in 1920 to be capable of believing in and serving in combat for a country that did not grant him the same full rights and privileges it did to others? How could that man then turn to his own sons and admonish them to follow his example of service?

The answer is simple: that man, my father Herman West Sr., believed in the words of Douglass. He believed that it was in the military that you could, as the US Army once said, "be all that you can be."

But somewhere along the way, we lost those voices in the black community that advocated for military service. We have also lost those who inspired me—the dads and men who challenged the young black men and women in the community to serve this nation. It is not my intention to sound an alarm of dismay, but we should have a degree of concern. Think about it: we have elevated black athletes to the position of role models. Recently, we have seen some of these role models take the position that America and our national symbols, such as the anthem and our flag, are not worthy of regard and respect. And these multimillionaire athletes will never face the overt, institutionalized racism faced by Jesse Owens and Jackie Robinson, who both broke the color line and defied the racial status quo by showing not only the United States of America but also the Nazi world of Hitler—who had his own agenda of proving that the Aryan race was superior even in sports—that black men are strong, determined, and capable. Owens won four track and field gold medals during the 1936 Summer Olympics in Berlin, setting a record that went unbroken for forty-eight years. Robinson made history as the first black man to play in Major League Baseball and was honored, among many other prizes and recognitions, with the National League Most Valuable Player Award in 1949.

Perhaps it is time for us to remember that the black community, like many American minority communities, saw military service as a means to achieving equality. It was not achieved by rioting or protesting but rather by proving equality through service, sacrifice, and commitment to the founding principles of this nation. It was believed that fighting for America would prove that we were not separate but equal. We were equal because a bullet from the enemies of freedom—of America—sees no color, no race. It only knows that its target is an American.

Now, I am quite sure the detractors and naysayers, if they have embarked upon reading this literary project, are already mocking the words I've said. It is not my intent to sugarcoat the oppressive nature of the past. What I do want to discuss, objectively, is why blacks sacrificed for so long. Why didn't they just give up or quit? In a way, no one would have blamed them for doing so.

Let's tell a few stories to remember those of the past, present, and future who have taken or will take the oath of enlistment to "support and defend the Constitution of the United States of America against all enemies, foreign and domestic, that they will bear true faith and allegiance to the same . . . that they take this obligation freely without any mental reservation or purpose of evasion . . . so help me God."

BLACK SERVICE TO AMERICA IN THE REVOLUTIONARY WAR AND THE WAR OF 1812

In March 1770, the first black man lost his life for what would become America. His name was Crispus Attucks, and he was a free man, a sailor. Not much is known about Attucks, but he is listed among those very first patriots to lose their lives for this nation. During the Revolutionary War, estimates say some nine thousand blacks served in the Continental Army. Some of them were signed over by their masters. Many had the expectation that their freedom would be earned by way of their service; they were gravely disappointed in the end.

The British also sought to exploit blacks' desire to be free, and in November of 1775, Virginia's Lord Dunmore issued a proclamation offering freedom to blacks who would join the British forces. This was in response to the formation of the Continental Army in June 1775, the

Continental Navy in October 1775, and, later, in November 1775, the Continental Marines.

Sadly, the hopes and dreams of freedom never came to fruition for the blacks who fought for an entire nation's freedom. It is a sad stain—one that the insidious idea of reparations cannot absolve—that a nation founded on the principle that all men are created equal failed to make all men free after gaining and winning its independence. However, for some odd reason, blacks remained hopeful.

The War of 1812 was the next test of whether America would honor freedom for blacks. It was round two against the British, who had taken to impounding American ships and sailors. Many people do not mention the War of 1812 beyond several memorable events. One, of course, was the British burning of the Capitol in Washington, DC. The other was the bombardment of Fort McHenry in Baltimore Harbor, which led to Francis Scott Key writing the words of the "Star-Spangled Banner," our national anthem. But the most memorable event of the War of 1812 actually came after the war was over: the Battle of New Orleans.

We used to sing this little song as part of army physical training runs:

In 1814 we took a little trip,
along with General Jackson down the Mighty Mississip,
We took a little bacon and we took a little beans,
and we met the bloody British at a place called New Orleans,

We fired our guns and the British kept a comin',
It wasn't quite as many as it was a while ago,
We fired once more and they began a runnin',
Straight down the Mississippi to the Gulf of Mexico.

Well, one of those units that fought with General Jackson was a militia unit called the Louisiana Battalion of Free Men. Upon the purchase of Louisiana, there had been an agreement that certain traditions were to be kept; one of those exemptions allowed for militia units of black freemen. Sadly, once again, after defeating the British, the freedom of America was not extended to all.

But, for some reason, blacks still remained hopeful.

In the intervening years between the War of 1812 and the Civil War, blacks did see service, mostly in the navy but primarily as servants to officers. Oddly enough, it was the very same Louisiana Battalion of Free Men that did service in the Mexican War.

The Civil War, Westward Expansion, and the Spanish-American War

The turning point came in the Civil War, specifically after the Battle of Antietam. There can be no debate about this point: the Civil War did not set out to end slavery. It was, without a doubt, centered on the growing belief that the southern states were independent and saw the US government and federal troops as usurpers and invaders. The firing upon Fort Sumter in Charleston, South Carolina, set forth events that would not be contained. The hero of Texas, the first president of the Republic of Texas, did not support Texas joining the Confederacy and predicted the South's loss. He lost his political office over his lack of support to the Confederacy.

President Lincoln wanted to walk a very tight rope in not forcing more border states into the arms of the Confederacy, so he did not challenge the issue of slavery.

It was not until the Battle of Antietam in 1862—the bloodiest day in US military history, with nearly twenty-two thousand killed—that Lincoln changed course. Antietam was actually a draw, militarily, but

Lincoln claimed it as a victory since they had forced General Robert E. Lee's Army of Northern Virginia to withdraw and abandon its goal of invading the North through Maryland. Lincoln knew that he had to capitalize on this perceived victory immediately. He had to shift public opinion against the Confederacy, and the best way possible for this to happen was to demonize the South and its institution of slavery.

And so, on January 1, 1863, President Abraham Lincoln issued the Emancipation Proclamation. Later, Lincoln would push for the Thirteenth Amendment, which officially ended slavery in the United States. But it was after Lincoln's Emancipation Proclamation that Frederick Douglass spoke the words that would set in motion the real quest for freedom, liberty, and equality for blacks in America.

And those words deserve to be repeated: "Once let the black man get upon his person the brass letter, US, let him get an eagle on his button, and a musket on his shoulder and bullets in his pocket, there is no power on earth that can deny that he has earned the right to citizenship."

It was Frederick Douglass who made it possible for blacks to finally and lawfully have a full unit under the arms of the US Army. A unit with its own designation and its own colors: the historic Fifty-Fourth Massachusetts Regiment. We all remember the Academy Award–winning movie *Glory*. Gotta tell y'all, I am tearing up right now thinking of the sacrifices those first men of color under the US flag went through.

Anytime I watch that movie, I shed tears of pride and honor because these men made it possible for the men of the West family to wear the uniform and the brass letters "US." And no, those men were not intended to be a combat unit, but they did fight at Fort Wagner, one of the forts defending the seaward path into Charleston Harbor. The first black Medal of Honor recipient was from the Fifty-Fourth Massachusetts, and since then, ninety black men have been awarded the prestigious Medal of Honor. One of them, Robert Augustus Sweeney, was a two-time recipient. Only nineteen men have ever achieved that feat.

The Fifty-Fourth Massachusetts opened the door with their valorous service. They did not have black commanding officers, but that would soon change.

It was not too long after the end of the Civil War that a former slave named Henry O. Flipper became the first black to attend the United States Military Academy at West Point. He was the first black commissioned officer in the United States of America—a forerunner for a simple kid from the Old Fourth Ward in Atlanta who would become an army officer on July 31, 1982, at the University of Tennessee. These days, so many talk about glass ceilings; the Fifty-Fourth Massachusetts Regiment and Henry O. Flipper should be highly esteemed in the black community for cracking that ceiling and paving the way for many to follow in uniformed service to our nation.

And so, as America moved past the Civil War with the Thirteenth, Fourteenth, and Fifteenth Amendments added to our Constitution to end slavery, make blacks citizens, and provide equal protection and rights, one would have thought all was well. Indeed, the immediate results was that blacks—Republicans—were seeking and attaining elected offices. Also, the number of all black units expanded from just the one, the Fifty-Fourth Massachusetts, to four more historic units: the Ninth and Tenth Cavalry—the famed Buffalo Soldiers—and the Twenty-Fourth and Twenty-Fifth Infantry Regiments.

Now, here is a little bit of black military trivia: Who was the first black woman to enlist in the US Army? Her name was Cathay Williams, born in 1844, and she is the American version of Mulan. She used the male pseudonym of William Cathay and served in the Thirty-Eighth Infantry Regiment from 1866 to 1868. Thanks to a black woman, we have already had a woman serving in a combat unit.

This history of the Buffalo Soldiers is renowned in the American West and Southwest. I would suggest that everyone visit the Buffalo Soldier Museum in Fort Huachuca, Arizona, known as the Home of the Buffalo

Soldier. The Buffalo Soldiers were the group in which young US Army lieutenant Henry O. Flipper served under the command of General Benjamin Grierson. And for those of you who wondered where US Army general John Pershing's nickname, "Blackjack," came from, it is because he commanded the black troops of the Ninth and Tenth Cavalry, who participated in the punitive expedition against Pancho Villa.

We all know that Teddy Roosevelt and his Rough Riders took San Juan Hill, but guess what? The black combat troops of the Twenty-Fourth and Twenty-Fifth Infantry Regiments were there also.

Yes, black army units. Yes, black graduates from West Point. Charles Young was the second. Yes, black units participating in the westward expansion of these United States, in a cross-border operation against Pancho Villa, and in deployment to a foreign combat theater of operations in Cuba after the sinking of the USS *Maine*, which had black sailors aboard. Blacks were now constitutionally regarded as citizens and had rights—constitutional rights, with equal protection under the law—but there was a dark specter looming in America.

The Republicans had lost control of the US House of Representatives and Senate in Washington, DC, and there were two new enemies that blacks had to face: Jim Crow and the Ku Klux Klan.

WORLD WAR I

The war to end all wars had been raging in the trenches for years in Europe. The United States had avoided engaging in the conflict over European nationalism for more than three years. Then came the German U-boat sinking of the American ship the *Lusitania*. It changed everything. We chose to send our "doughboys" over there, and once again, blacks stepped up to the plate to serve this nation at a brutal time of Jim Crow segregation.

The most well known black unit of World War I consisted of the famed "Harlem Hellfighters," the 369th Infantry Regiment. The general of the army, John "Blackjack" Pershing, who had once commanded black cavalry troops, now had to figure out what to do with an all-black infantry regiment. Pershing chose to send the entire unit to the French, along with a certain admonition to not show them any equal—and certainly not preferential—treatment. The French did nothing of the sort; they allowed the 369th to fully fight in the French sector, earning high honors, such as the French Croix de Guerre. This, of course, did not settle well with General Pershing or with America.

These American combat heroes returned not to triumph but to what would become a scourge upon America: racial animosity and lynchings. It became the objective of white racists, supremacists, and others to ensure that these black men were not afforded the right to be armed and defend themselves. There were many notable race riots in America against blacks returning from World War I. I know because one occurred in the same city where I attended college and was commissioned as an army officer: Knoxville, Tennessee.

Yes, blacks had served this nation in overseas combat operations twice. They had constitutional rights, but they did not have societal or cultural rights. Yet they kept believing.

WORLD WAR II

The black community in America was aware of the racist policies of Adolf Hitler and Nazi Germany. Doggone, ya think someone could have had a bullet with Hitler's name on it in World War I, when he was just a corporal. There was no doubt that blacks saw Hitler as a threat even as they fought for equality here in America. And when the Japanese attacked Pearl Harbor, blacks had a hero of their own from that "day that shall live in infamy": Doris Miller. As with most blacks in the navy, Miller had been relegated to service duty in the galley. But on that day, Miller manned an antiaircraft gun and shot down Japanese aircraft.

Blacks started off in support roles in World War II. I am quite sure there was once again a fear of having all-black combat units that could prove their equality, their value, and their valor. But, of course, blacks didn't remain in those support roles throughout the war. There was another major breakthrough, cracking the glass ceiling.

At Tuskegee, there would be a revolutionary development. It was an endeavor chided, scorned, and frowned upon. It was pushed for by Eleanor Roosevelt, the First Lady of the United States, mainly due to her relationship with astute black educator Mary McLeod Bethune. That endeavor would be known as the Tuskegee Airmen—the "Red Tails." White racists and supremacists didn't believe that blacks could be fighter pilots. However, at Tuskegee, Booker T. Washington established an institution that fostered a can-do attitude that determined one's altitude—literally, in this case.

Young black men from all over flocked to join this unit, and thanks to a trailblazer named General Benjamin O. Davis Sr., his own son, Benjamin O. Davis Jr., would become an American fighter pilot—reminiscent of the challenge my dad, a World War II veteran, would give to me, his middle son. Yes, they did; they became the 332nd Fighter Group, and in World War II, they never lost a bomber under their escort. I had the distinguished honor of having a Tuskegee Airman—William "Stickey" Jackson, my dad's friend from back in Alabama—as my godfather. We have to challenge young black men in our communities to strive for something greater. We must utilize the living role models and heroes they have in their lives.

Those brave men of Tuskegee proved that blacks had not just the physical capacity but also the mental and intellectual capacity to be warriors of the air. From this endeavor came great black aviators such as General Benjamin O. Davis Jr., General Daniel "Chappie" James, and General Frank Peterson, a Marine Corps fighter pilot.

We would also witness a new era of black combat units in the army, including the 761st Tank Destroyer Battalion and the 452nd Anti-Aircraft Artillery Battalion. We would also have the first black marines, the Montford Point Marines. As a US congressman, I was honored to be a part of their Congressional Gold Medal presentation in the US Capitol because my older brother was a marine.

All of the success, the tenacity, and the perseverance of these men of color who served during World War II finally paid off. President Harry Truman signed Executive Order 9981 in 1948, desegregating the US Armed Forces.

From the death of Crispus Attucks in 1770 to desegregation in 1948, it took blacks 178 years to finally stand side by side with whites in service and defense of these United States of America. That led to the landmark *Brown v. Board of Education* decision, which would end the policy of "separate but equal." Not too long afterward came the Civil Rights Act of 1964.

But there were still obstacles to overcome. Many felt that in Vietnam, blacks were thrown into the cauldron of combat and used up. Just so y'all know, my elder brother was not drafted into the marines; he volunteered and joined the infantry of his own accord. From that point forward, however, voices in the black community stopped speaking of service to the country.

Today, too many of our young, fatherless black males have no direction, no sense of belonging to something of honor. You probably remember the movie *Men of Honor*, which told the story of the US Navy's first salvage diver, Command Master Chief Carl Brashear. That is the level of perseverance, character, and honor we need restored into the black community.

Let me just close this chapter by listing some of the impeccable black men in uniform who have made a difference in my life: Corporal Herman West Sr. (my dad). Lance Corporal Herman West Jr. (my elder brother). Master Sergeant Ronald Keith Graham (my father-in-law). General Lloyd Austin III. General Vincent Brooks. General Dennis Via. Major General Rodney Anderson. Major General Byron Bagby. Brigadier General Leo Brooks. Command Sergeant Major Norris Hand and Command Sergeant Major Larry Taylor. Major Henry Burns, 2–20th FA Regiment (my battalion command sergeant). Command Sergeant Major Tyrone Massey (US Army Special Forces, my senior enlisted army ROTC instructor, University of Tennessee). Medal of Honor recipient Sergeant First Class Melvin Morris. Sergeant First Class David McMichael (my HSJROTC instructor).

Today, the names continue, and I am proud to mention my own nephew, US Army Major Herman Bernard West III, who carries on the legacy of West men who have worn the brass button with US upon their chest.

The real advancement of equality for blacks in America came from men and women who took an oath to support and defend. And they should forever be our true role models, not the athletes, the entertainers, the rap artists, or the gang members.

Like my dad told me at age fifteen, there is no greater honor than to wear the uniform of the United States of America. For a young black boy or girl, it is an extraordinary legacy.

PART II

OUR HISTORY FROM EXECUTIVE ORDER 9981 TO THE COMMUNITY REINVESTMENT ACT

CHAPTER SEVEN

THE IDEOLOGICAL SHIFT OF THE BLACK COMMUNITY

As we've just witnessed, the black community successfully came together and supported each other during the worst time in the history of the United States of America: slavery. Black men and women would gather in churches to find inner strength, purpose, and hope for a better future. They would help each other learn how to read and write because, as Frederick Douglass quickly understood, education was the only way to gain freedom—not only physically but also spiritually and mentally. Black-owned businesses could count on the support of their own communities, thus allowing black fathers and mothers to thrive and provide their children with better opportunities for their future. Church, family, education, and business acumen were at the center of black America, which embraced conservative values and relied on the Republican Party and its principles, trusting in their mission to help black Americans finally be recognized as citizens of the country they helped build with great pride. Indeed, during the hardest and most challenging time in the history of our country, the black community found refuge and support in the core values of the party of Lincoln—the party that finally ended slavery.

Today, however, the black community is witnessing a different type of slavery than the sinful stealing of African bodies whipped into building this country. Through their own votes, black people eagerly shackle themselves and, with big grins, happily hand whips to progressive socialists, begging to be beaten into an ideological servitude.

Why are blacks voting for the party that gives them stuff—thus enticing them into economic enslavement—as opposed to the party that has proven throughout history to be the one that truly has their best interests at heart? What happens when America's concessions to black folk marinate into control over black folk? Our fight, then, is no longer against flesh and blood but against hidden agendas and principalities.

In 1963, Malcolm X warned us when he said: "The white liberal differs from the white conservative only in one way: the liberal is more deceitful than the conservative. The liberal is more hypocritical than the conservative. Both want power, but the white liberal is the one who has perfected the art of posing as the Negro's friend and benefactor; and by winning the friendship, allegiance, and support of the Negro, the white liberal is able to use the Negro as a pawn or tool in this political 'football game' that is constantly raging between the white liberals and the white conservatives. Politically the American Negro is nothing but a football."[1]

Black people have to realize that there's a fine line between equality of opportunity and equality of outcome, between a hand up and a handout, between civil rights and surrendered rights. In our modern day, that line is the difference between freedom and slavery.

What follows is a look back at when the ideological and political shift in the black community happened. When and why did the black community choose to side with the Democratic Party even though, historically, the Republican Party was always the one to fight for their freedom and rights?

To answer this question, I will focus on several presidents who, in their own way, addressed the disparity that existed—and still exists—in American society between black and white people.

CHAPTER EIGHT

PRESIDENT TRUMAN AND
THE DESEGREGATION OF THE ARMED FORCES

There's no definitive time stamp that we can use as the start of the ideological shift in the black community. But to keep from writing a never-ending book, I'll start with Harry S. Truman's presidency from the mid-1940s through the early 1950s.

Truman inherited a country from President Franklin D. Roosevelt with nearly thirteen million black men and women who were no longer silent and invisible.[1] America could not afford to keep ignoring the aftershocks of institutional racism, especially the Jim Crow laws in the South.

For all its flaws, Roosevelt's New Deal suite of programs at least put race relations on center stage. Roosevelt had led a political party that was heavily represented in Congress by Southern Democrats who supported segregation and even opposed the adoption of federal antilynching laws. And yet, black Americans felt validated by Roosevelt's rhetoric and saw a glimpse of hope that perhaps they could indeed be recognized as equals. The New Deal "ushered in a new political climate in which Afro-Americans and their allies could begin to struggle with some expectation of success."[2] Millions of black Americans felt as though Roosevelt had given them hope for a world where black America was no longer invisible, one where black America was as important as white America, one where black America finally had a future. They believed in him so much that many of them named their children after FDR or hung his photo in their living rooms, and 68 percent of them rushed to vote for the Democratic Party in 1940 in order to have him as their president—a staggering number, considering that in just 1932, 70 percent of black America had voted for Herbert Hoover in what would eventually become the last time a significant amount of black Americans voted for the Republican Party.[3] Black Americans became enticed with the possibility, with the hope, with the dream of *what it would be like, if only*. They were duped into believing that the Democratic Party had their best interests at heart. Even though the New Deal failed to "end the rampant discrimination against blacks in the North . . . to enfranchise black southerners, to eradicate segregation, or to elevate the great mass of blacks who remained a submerged caste of menials, sharecroppers, unskilled laborers, and domestics," it had succeeded in providing black people with that glimpse of hope that maybe, just maybe, things could change one day.[4]

That hope was fueled even more by Truman, who—listening to his assistant and counsel Clark Clifford, who warned him that "unless there are new and real efforts . . . the Negro bloc . . . will go Republic"[5]—began providing black America with concrete results and not just empty promises. He made black people feel like their voices had finally been heard when he addressed black voters in Harlem—the capital of black America—in an unprecedented move by a presidential candidate. This strategy secured him ninety thousand votes from the black community in Harlem, while his opponent, Republican candidate Thomas Dewey, secured only twenty-five thousand.[6] This was a clear sign that black America had abandoned the party of Lincoln.

During Truman's presidency, which gives us a look at the country in the post–World War II, pre–*Brown v. Board of Education* era, we start to see more efforts to promote equality of opportunity—rather than equality of outcome—in areas ranging from bus travel to baseball. For example, in 1946, the US Supreme Court ruled that segregation on interstate buses was unconstitutional. But President Truman's legacy will forever be tied to his 1948 Executive Order 9981, which desegregated the armed forces.

In *Harry Truman and Civil Rights: Moral Courage and Political Risks*, Michael Gardner argues that unlike President Roosevelt before him and presidents Kennedy and Johnson after him, Truman pushed for equality of opportunity without any immediate pressure or crisis.[7] His platform was "to do what he felt was morally right."[8] Politics was a secondary concern.

To be sure, politics typically plays a part in presidential decisions, at least on some level. In November 1946, the Democrats soundly lost the midterm elections. A few weeks later, Truman established the President's Committee on Civil Rights (PCCR).[9] It took courage, yes, but the timing wasn't a coincidence. In October 1947, PCCR published its landmark report *To Secure These Rights*.

Though often overlooked, this document, with its thirty-five recommendations, laid the foundation for civil rights for the next fifty years. *To Secure These Rights* called for federal antilynching laws, jury reform, elimination of the poll tax, and, most notably, the desegregation of the military.

Gardner calls the PCCR report "tantamount to a political declaration of war against Southern Democrats."[10] It was a "politically reckless" move that almost cost Truman the 1948 election against Thomas Dewey, a Republican governor from New York.[11]

Truman became an unlikely civil rights advocate, given his family history and political background, coming from the border state of Missouri. He actually needed the black vote for the 1948 election since he didn't get help from the Dixiecrats, led by Strom Thurmond from South Carolina.

Truman also needed to send a global message. The United States had recently signed the United Nations charter and would soon establish NATO.[12] The country needed to be seen as a dependable partner that would keep its commitments to human rights and to its allies.

His June 29, 1947, speech to the NAACP at the Lincoln Memorial in Washington, DC, is worth reading.[13] In it, he stood for values and principles that are at the core of conservatism, thus resonating as familiar and reassuring to the ears and hearts of black America. For example, he pushed for equality of opportunity, not outcome. He allowed the black community to stand equal to the white community in protecting our country against a common enemy. He directly undercut the institutional racism promoted by the Southern Democrats, placing himself in a vulnerable place within his own political party, in order to do what was right by black America. For these reasons and more, I would argue that Truman was a conservative.

> As Americans, we believe that every man should be free to live his life as he wishes. He should be limited only by his responsibility to his fellow countrymen. If this freedom is to be more than a dream, each man must be guaranteed equality of opportunity. The only limit to an American's achievement should be his ability, his industry, and his character. Our immediate task is to remove the last remnants of the barriers which stand between millions of our citizens and their birthright. There is no justifiable reason for discrimination because of ancestry, or religion, or race, or color.[14]

I can't overstate the importance of the PCCR's recommendation for desegregating the military, summarized in Executive Order 9981. Blacks have played a critical role in the United States Armed Forces since the American Revolution. A slave known as Prince Easterbrooks is recorded as one of the first casualties at the Battle of Concord.[15] Thousands of blacks—free and enslaved—fought alongside white men during that war.

New York civil rights leader Asa Philip Randolph is believed to have been a key voice in Truman's ear to desegregate the military.[16] In addition, in April 1946, a review board chaired by General Alvan Gillem Jr.

advised that the US Army's policy should be to "eliminate, at the earliest practicable moment, any special consideration based on race."[17] General Gillem mentioned to Truman that the army already had desegregated its hospitals because of the unnecessary cost and inefficiency created by maintenance of separate facilities for white and black patients.[18]

By October 1953, the army announced that it had integrated more than 90 percent of black troops in its ranks.[19]

There is a reason that a portrait of President Truman hangs proudly in our home in Garland, Texas, and always shall. It is not just that Truman was an artillery officer in World War I—although his being a fellow Redleg does establish him in a league of his own. It is not just his immediate recognition of the modern-day State of Israel in 1948. No, it is because I have always looked up to men and women who took a stand for freedom and were not afraid to sacrifice their position, status, or even life to change the present for the betterment of future generations. In his order to desegregate the armed forces of the United States, President Truman actually set the stage for the proverbial wall called "separate but equal" to come down. Finally, the dream that had started with the first black men to wear the uniform of the United States, the Fifty-Fourth Massachusetts Regiment, came to be. Blacks would serve side by side with whites in service to this constitutional republic.

I was not there, since I was not born until 1961, but I can only imagine the excitement for my dad, Buck West. During the time of Truman's executive order, my dad had just finished serving his country as Corporal Herman West in World War II. I can also imagine the jubilation of my godfather, William "Sticky" Jackson, a Tuskegee Airman.

Finally, after all those years of withstanding disrespect and disregard, American black servicemen and women would be able to stand shoulder to shoulder on freedom's ramparts with whites. Though it wasn't an easy transition, we first saw in the Korean War how blacks and whites could fight side by side against our country's enemies.

Of course, racism did not suddenly disappear, but there would now be a precedent, a monumental case study against racial prejudices. My elder brother still faced the sting of racist attitudes from some whites as a marine in the Vietnam War. However, Lance Corporal Herman West Jr. would serve in a US Marine Corps that would have black officers in commanding roles, and not just of black units.

As a child, one of my military heroes was the first black Marine Corps fighter pilot, Lieutenant General Frank Peterson Jr., who passed in August 2015. Thanks to President Truman, we could actually begin the final push to bring to fruition Jefferson's words: "We hold these truths to be self-evident, that all Men are created equal." And in being created equal, we have equality of opportunity on a level playing field to achieve, excel, and pursue our desired happiness. And the real equality for blacks in America had to start where it was most important: with those willing to give the last full measure of devotion to this great country.

And so it was for me back at the age of fifteen, when former US Army Corporal Herman West Sr. said to his middle son these immortal words: "Boy, there is no greater honor than to wear the uniform of this country. In the military, no one can hold you back because of your skin color. You can rise and achieve what you want to become. I want you to be the first officer in our family."

On July 31, 1982, at the University of Tennessee, my father's charge was fulfilled. I became Second Lieutenant Allen Bernard West, US Army Field Artillery. Not only that; in the subsequent generation, Corporal Buck West's grandson is also a US Army Field Artillery officer, Major Herman Bernard West III.

Truman's Executive Order 9981 made all of this possible for the men of the West family. His action rewarded my dad for his service to this nation and inspired him to ensure his progeny would follow his impeccable example of combat service to America. "Give 'em Hell"

Harry, a field artillery officer, broke down the barriers and enabled me to become an army artillery officer, just as he had been. And that is why for as long as I live, President Harry Truman's image will be proudly displayed in my home.

CHAPTER NINE

PRESIDENT EISENHOWER'S CIVIL RIGHTS LEGACY

Dwight D. Eisenhower was one of the country's finest military men—that's not up for debate. He was supreme commander of the Allied forces in Western Europe during World War II, leading the invasion of Nazi-occupied Europe on June 6, 1944.

What is debatable among historians was his stance on civil rights. As president, he carried out Truman's executive order to desegregate the military. Certainly, he knew the value of a desegregated military in America's upcoming Cold War challenges after World War II. However, he showed an indifference to Mamie Till's pleas for support in the wake of her son Emmett's lynching after he supposedly whistled at a white woman. And he declined requests from Martin Luther King Jr. to "lend the weight of his great office" to end the "state of terror" in the South.[1] Mobs were harassing black children, black churches were being burned, and activists were being murdered. Eisenhower said, "I don't know what another speech would do about the thing right now."[2]

"You cannot change people's hearts merely by laws," Eisenhower said. In the address at Western Michigan University, December 18, 1963, Martin Luther King Jr. would respond by saying: "It may be true that the law cannot change the heart, but it can restrain the heartless. It may be true that the law cannot make a man love me, but it can keep him from lynching me and I think that is pretty important, also. So, there is a need for executive orders. There is a need for judicial decrees. There is a need for civil rights legislation on the local scale within states and on the national scale from the federal government."

Roy Wilkins, a former executive director of the NAACP, said, "President Eisenhower was a fine general and a good, decent man, but if he had fought World War II the way he fought for civil rights, we would all be speaking German now."[3]

I don't completely agree with Wilkins's critique because it overlooks one of the bravest acts of presidential leadership in our nation's history. In fact, President Eisenhower—who embraced and stood for many conservative values and principles, including limited power to the federal government in order to favor individual initiatives—took many actions that clearly showed where he stood when it came to the fight for civil rights. For example, he desegregated the nation's capital and had Hollywood executives open up their theaters to both whites and blacks indiscriminately. He also appointed judges who would grant the civil rights movement some of its most important victories. He appointed Earl Warren as chief justice of the Supreme Court that ultimately decided to desegregate schools in the *Brown v. Board of Education* ruling. Could it be that the reason history doesn't always remember Ike as a civil rights hero is because he rarely sought credit for what he did?

Eisenhower clearly preferred to make decisions—even those that might be unpopular with a core voting block of southern voters—rather than deliver speeches. For example, on September 25, 1957, President Eisenhower ordered the 101st Airborne Division to Little Rock not only to disperse the mob but to escort the Little Rock Nine—a group of nine black students who enrolled in the previously all-white Central High School—to school. It is impossible for me to overstate the impact of that decision. The testimony from one of those black students says it all.

"I went in not through the side doors, but up the front stairs, and there was a feeling of pride and hope that yes, this is the United States; yes, there is a reason I salute the flag; and it's going to be okay," said Melba Pattillo Beals, recalling events that day.[4] And mind you, Eisenhower didn't perceive this as a victory. Rather, he saw the fact that he was forced to deploy troops to ensure the safety of black children going to school as a major defeat. To know that racial tensions in his country had come down to that produced an overwhelming sadness in his life.

So, if we care to look closely at his two terms as president, Eisenhower had the strongest record on civil rights since Reconstruction. "He made substantial progress in the area of civil rights, more than any other individual president between Lincoln and Johnson," said Michael Mayer, a University of Montana history professor.[5]

When you hold a political office, especially that of president, you are put on public display for both reverence and ridicule. Eisenhower, like most political leaders, wrestled with a multiplicity of decisions unknown to outsiders. Those decisions were more than a simple dichotomy of good and evil; often, they were embedded in a quagmire of consequences.

It is our responsibility as an electorate to vote for our leaders based on their adherence to governing principles. And that's why 40 percent of the black community voted for Eisenhower, showing their support for the party of Lincoln—the party that had always stood by their side and made sure they were given equal opportunities, not outcomes.[6] One of the main differences between conservatives and progressive socialists is that the former believe in protecting each individual's opportunity to succeed, while the latter believe in having the government provide them with the same outcome, thus rewarding everybody the same way.

Eisenhower was a man of action and not one of many words—as opposed to the Democratic Party and their empty promises to the black community. He was also the silent-leader type, the one who acts behind the curtain, even at the risk of being misjudged as an uncaring and distant person—as happened when he did not publicly address the killing of Emmett Till or the bombing of Martin Luther King's house.

Eisenhower was a man of faith and a kindred spirit who, during a chat with Booker T. Washington's daughter Portia Washington Pittman, asserted that "while we have to change the hearts of men, we cannot do it by cold lawmaking, but must make these changes by appealing to reason, by prayer, and by constantly working at it through our own efforts."[7] Like Washington—a man Eisenhower looked up to and admired—when it came to the fight for racial equality, he believed in gradualism, and, as the pragmatic leader he was, he moved slowly yet firmly in silently accomplishing his goals to ensure that black people had the same rights as white people.

After Pittman confessed to him that she regretted her father had not lived long enough to see some of his dreams for racial equality come true, Eisenhower replied, "Most men who make a real contribution to civilization do not live long enough to see their work bear fruit. While they are living they have to get the satisfaction of knowing that what they are trying to do may sometime mean something to mankind."[8]

And just like my mentor Washington, Eisenhower did not live long enough to see that all his hard—and silent—work would pave the way for more progress in the fight for racial equality. However, he was able to witness his administration solidify the Republican Party's commitment to the advancement of civil rights by fighting for equal opportunities for all.

CHAPTER TEN

PRESIDENT KENNEDY AND THE NEW BLACK DEMOCRATS

The voting patterns of black Americans started to shift toward Democrats once again with the presidency of John F. Kennedy. Though in office for only less than three years before he was assassinated, Kennedy routinely hosted blacks at White House events and strategically appointed a select few to prominent positions, most notably Thurgood Marshall to the federal bench.

Unlike Eisenhower, Kennedy was more outspoken and presented himself as a friend of blacks and a sympathizer to their struggle for equality. Let's stop here for a moment, shall we? Pay close attention to the words I used to describe Kennedy in the previous sentence: *outspoken* and *presented himself.* Kennedy's political campaign was very much one of *appearance* rather than *substance.* Eisenhower was a man of a few words; he preferred to have his actions speak for him. Kennedy, on the other hand, preferred to talk, to entice the black community with his oratory skills, and then, when it came down to it, he never worked to advance the fight for racial equality. And yet, black America loved him. "Even though he would leave no new civil rights laws as his legacy, JFK nevertheless captured the heart of black America, becoming the best-loved chief executive in history," said former *Jet* and *Ebony* civil rights correspondent Simeon Booker in his book *Shocking the Conscience: A Reporter's Account of the Civil Rights Movement.*

The love affair started with Kennedy's election. A *Jet* poll in August 1959 showed black Democratic voters split among presidential contenders Adlai Stevenson, JFK, and Hubert Humphrey.[1] Humphrey was a devout civil rights advocate and very outspoken on the subject, but he lacked the money and political skills of JFK. In January 1960, when Humphrey announced his candidacy, his office failed to alert the black press, "and not a single Negro showed up to hear the most liberal contender make his bid."[2]

"Massachusetts Senator Kennedy, meanwhile, had telegrammed invitations to each Negro press representative to hear him on the civil rights question," Booker said.

Republican leaders could sense the shift in the black vote. They took out a two-page ad in the *Montgomery Advertiser* accusing Democrats of supporting civil rights in the North and white supremacy down in the South. The ad asked, "Where Do Democrats Really Stand?" opposite an invitation—emblazoned with "White Supremacy" logos—to meet Senator Lyndon Johnson and Lady Bird Johnson at a campaign stop in the Alabama capital.[3]

On the campaign trail, Kennedy hopscotched across the country, catering to the black press. "Kennedy's speeches were so literate and generalized, so lofty and principled, that no one could take offense," Booker said. Seemingly overnight, Kennedy transformed himself from a conservative to a man sympathetic to civil rights. He made sure that a black newsman took his turn as a pool reporter on his private plane.[4]

According to many political historians, what likely sealed the black vote for Democrats was Kennedy's telephone call to Coretta Scott King after her husband was arrested in Atlanta and jailed on a traffic violation. That phone call became international news. In contrast, Richard Nixon, who was running as the Republican candidate, was advised to issue a statement or take some sort of action, but his aides thought it was a "bad strategy."[5] Nixon, as a candidate, did nothing, and black America took note.

The Kennedys doubled down on their support. Robert Kennedy contacted the mayor of Atlanta and publicly appealed for King's release. Meanwhile, Nixon, still refusing to speak out, came across as hostile and insensitive to the civil rights movement. Once King was released, he stated that he was indebted to Senator Kennedy, and even though King did not endorse a political party, black Americans interpreted his words as a clear sign that the Democratic Party was on their side. Meanwhile, behind closed doors, the Kennedy campaign sought to cash in on this strategic move by printing "tens of thousands of pamphlets describing the episode and distributed them in black churches across the country on the Sunday before the election."[6] The result? A staggering 78 percent of black voters clearly wanted Kennedy as their president.[7]

For decades later in most black homes, it was common to see three pictures on the wall: Jesus, Martin Luther King Jr., and John Fitzgerald Kennedy. Kennedy won that 1960 election, securing the majority of the black vote, but it's debatable whether he truly deserved it. A closer look at Kennedy's campaign shows that he put up a winning façade by talking his way into black people's hearts, but behind that curtain—the same one used by Eisenhower to actually act on civil rights progress by fighting for equal opportunities—his eloquent rhetoric was hollow. In fact, behind that curtain, he was "urging King to end his nonviolent protests."[8] For example, when asked if he was for or against the March on Washington, Kennedy answered, "We want success in the Congress . . . not a big show on the Capitol." To that, A. Philip Randolph replied, "The Negroes are already in the streets."[9]

If we lift that veil of convincing chatter and zoom in even more on Kennedy's hollow promises, we see that he had few blacks on his speaking circuit and virtually none employed on his campaign. Kennedy's political shiftiness was even more evident on Election Night in November 1960 in Hyannis Port, Massachusetts. A group of elite black Kennedy supporters went to await the results with the other upper echelon of supporters but were initially denied admittance to the facility because they lacked credentials.[10]

"The most expensive Negro vote-getting organization in history collapsed suddenly . . . Its job was done," Booker said.

Black politicians were lining up for jobs after the election but were largely shut out except for a few named to minor posts, such as Andrew Hatcher, hired as associate press secretary, which for many blacks was a symbol of success. Given Kennedy's untimely death, we will never know if things would have turned out differently had he stayed in office longer. We will never know if he would have acted on his beautiful words and actually done something concrete about civil rights and the fight for racial equality. While we could go on and on about the *what ifs,* the reality is clear: all that is left after Kennedy's presidency is seductive rhetoric—which had enticed the black community away from the Republican Party—of a better tomorrow that did not come true.

CHAPTER ELEVEN

PRESIDENT JOHNSON'S OPPORTUNISTIC BEHAVIOR

In a sense, civil rights laws and advancements have come by hook or crook. No one truly knows how these political leaders felt about blacks or why they made the decisions they did to further the movement. Truman had little political motivation to desegregate the military, but he did it anyway because it was the right thing to do. Eisenhower bravely escorted little black children to school with the 101st Airborne Division in Little Rock, and Kennedy, who passed no meaningful civil rights legislation and placed racist Democrats in positions above blacks, is put on a pedestal above them all because of tactical messaging and public relations.

After Kennedy's assassination, Lyndon Baines Johnson—a Southern Democrat who reportedly had a proclivity for peppering conversations with "nigger"—became president. Johnson was a civil rights opportunist who leveraged the movement for his party's political gain.

When defending his decision to appoint the very first black American man, Thurgood Marshall—a grandson of slaves—to the Supreme Court over a lesser known black judge not connected to the civil rights cause, Johnson said, "Son, when I appoint a nigger to the court, I want everyone to know he's a nigger."[1]

Doris Kearns Goodwin, a former Harvard historian and Johnson staffer, recalls LBJ explaining his political position on the civil rights movement to Senator Richard Russell Jr. (D-GA): "These Negroes, they're getting pretty uppity these days and that's a problem for us since they've got something now they never had before, the political pull to back up their uppityness. Now we've got to do something about this, we've got to give them a little something, just enough to quiet them down, not enough to make a difference."[2]

Political historians note that Johnson often would ramp up the bigoted language when trying to win over prosegregation Dixicrat colleagues. According to Johnson biographer Robert Caro, he would adjust his pronunciation of "nigger" by region, using "nigra" with some southern legislators and "negra" with others. Discussing civil rights legislation with men like Mississippi Democrat James Eastland, who committed most of his life to defending white supremacy, he'd simply call it "the nigger bill."[3]

Then, in 1957, Johnson helped pass the "nigger bill," known to most as the Civil Rights Act of 1957. With the 1964 Civil Rights Act and the 1965 Voting Rights Act, the segregationists would go to their graves knowing the cause they'd given their lives to had been betrayed by a man they believed to be one of their own. When Caro asked segregationist Georgia Democrat Herman Talmadge how he felt when Johnson, signing the Civil Rights Act, said, "We shall overcome," Talmadge said, "Sick."[4]

On page 33 of Ronald Kessler's 1995 book *Inside the White House: The Hidden Lives of the Modern Presidents and the Secrets of the World's Most Powerful Institution*, the author says that on one trip, Johnson was discussing his proposed civil rights bill with two governors. In explaining why it was so important to him, he said it was simple: "I'll have them niggers voting Democratic for two hundred years." Kessler quotes the account of the conversation from Robert MacMillan, an Air Force One steward who was within earshot of the conversation. Unfortunately for us, Johnson seems to have been right.

However, if we look closely to the Civil Rights Act, we can see that it actually had a higher percentage of Republican votes than Democratic votes. More than 80 percent of Republicans in both houses voted in favor of the bill, compared to about 60 percent of

Democrats—thus proving yet again that the party of Lincoln has always had our bets interest at heart.[5] The division was more pronounced when split down the lines of which states were once were part of the Union or of the Confederacy during the Civil War era. Among former Union states, 90 percent of the House and 92 percent of the Senate voted for the bill. Among the former Confederate states, 8 percent of the House and 5 percent of the Senate voted for the bill.

The Civil Rights Act of 1964 was one part of a series of initiatives under LBJ's "Great Society" platform. The stated goal of the Great Society was to eliminate poverty and racial injustice. The unstated goal was to secure the minority vote for generations to come. The Congressional Research Service notes that in 1962, before the Great Society initiative began, mandatory spending was only 30 percent of the federal budget. Today that figure is nearly 60 percent and climbing.[6] All told, by the fiftieth anniversary of the Great Society in 2014, the program had cost America nearly $22 trillion.[7]

The Great Society proposals and President Jimmy Carter's Community Reinvestment Act—which would be signed a decade later in 1977—were catalysts to further shift the ideologies of black folk from conservatism to progressive socialism.

Let me be clear: I believe the stated goals of programs and policies like these are honorable. No one will argue that eliminating job discrimination, public segregation, and racist voter qualification practices was wrong. Our nation—my family included—is better because of it.

Herein lies the benefit of writing a book versus having the progressive socialist left twist my words into a sound bite or headline: "Lt. Col. Allen West disagrees with the Civil Rights Act of 1964," or "Black Conservative leader doesn't want equality" (or voter rights, home ownership, health care for the poor and elderly—take your pick). To that, I say: bovine excrement!

That's what the left does: they put anyone who opposes their agenda into a box because they're afraid that when people intelligently pick apart *all* of their proposals, they'll uncover hidden problems and costs.

Whenever I'm being interviewed on television or radio, delivering speeches, or writing like I'm doing now, my goal is to get the audience to view policies through the rubric of equality of opportunity versus equality of outcome. I want them to see how certain policy initiatives are being used to gain power and slowly siphon freedoms away from disenfranchised people. I want them to stop being hooked on immediate gratification and instead think about how these proposals will play out thirty to fifty years from now.

In a broad sense, the new Civil Rights Act dismantled Jim Crow laws, outlawed discrimination in public places, and banned discrimination based on race, gender, religion, or national origin by employers. All great things. But President Johnson went further—arguably too far.

I could really devote a separate book to the gross overreach of some Great Society programs. In all, Congress implemented 226 of President Johnson's 252 legislative requests by the end of his term. In five years, the American government pretty much doubled its regulatory role. Because of the Great Society's laws and programs, the federal government became a main source of funding for public schools, health care, parks, and radio. The government became our nanny, telling us what's safe to eat, how we should be entertained, and what private data to share. And that's when the black community, enticed by seductive political rhetoric filled with promises of a better tomorrow and blinded by shiny objects swinging in front of their eyes, began getting closer and closer to economic enslavement. Johnson's Great Society presented a strategy for the war on poverty that "focused on handouts that discourage self-improvement [and] caused more harm than help to the poor."

According to black activist Derryck Green, Johnson's administration and "the disastrous effects of the government's management of antipoverty initiatives are recognizable across racial lines, but the destruction is particularly evident in the black community. It effectively subsidized the dissolution of the black family by rendering the black man's role as a husband and a father irrelevant, invisible and—more specifically—disposable. The result has been several generations of blacks born into broken homes and broken communities experiencing social, moral and economic chaos. It fosters an inescapable dependency that primarily, and oftentimes solely, relies on government to sustain livelihoods."[8]

Many of the issues that we as black people face today, many of the problems that are tearing us apart, started when we were seduced by an enchanting sound—like the one made by the mythological sirens to entice sailors only to then kill them—of Johnson's War on Poverty.

CHAPTER TWELVE

THE MOYNIHAN MIND-SET

I believe that many costly progressive socialist programs were started with a sincere heart. At some point, the bleeding-heart liberal policy wonks had a sudden realization of the dreadful impact of decades of discriminatory practices. Their data clearly showed rising black poverty, unemployment, juvenile delinquency, drug use, broken families, and widening educational disparities.

Chief among them was Daniel Patrick Moynihan, an assistant secretary of labor for President Johnson. Intellectual liberals like Moynihan in the early 1960s wholeheartedly believed in proactive governmental action to improve the quality of life.[1] Moynihan stood out among this group after having reached success in early 1963 from producing a report titled *One-Third of a Nation*, which documented the high percentages of black men in single-parent families who failed mental and physical tests for the military draft.[2] In addition, Moynihan wrote a book with Harvard sociologist Nathan Glazer titled *Beyond the Melting Pot*, which focused on the power of family, ethnic, racial, and religious identifications in American life.[3]

Moynihan was the architect behind much of President Johnson's War on Poverty in 1964. He felt more needed to be done to help black Americans reach a socioeconomic status equal to whites. In an April 1964 memo to Labor Secretary Willard Wirtz, Moynihan wrote: "The Negroes are asking for unequal treatment. More seriously, it may be that without unequal treatment, there is no way for them to achieve anything like equal status in the long run."[4]

The line of thinking expressed in that memo led Moynihan to write his now famous report, *The Negro Family: The Case for National Action.* He started the research in January of 1965. Three months and seventy-eight pages later, he was done. In March 1965, the Labor Department printed one hundred copies of his work.[5]

The report, which on the title page read, "For Official Use Only," was never intended for the general public. It was aimed at White House officials. In distributing the report, he sent a message directed at President Johnson that read, "Equal opportunity for Negroes does not produce equal results—because the Negroes today are a grievously injured people who in fair and equal competition will by and large lose out." Later in the memo, Moynihan reminded Johnson: "You were born poor. You were brought up poor. Yet you came of age full of ambition, energy, and ability. Because your father and mother gave it to you. The richest inheritance any child can have is a stable, loving, disciplined family life."

The Negro Family cut to the chase in its opening line: "The United States is approaching a new crisis in race relations."[6] Throughout the report, there's a steady pleading to go beyond the recently passed Civil Rights Act of 1964: "Being Americans, they will now expect that in the near future equal opportunities for them as a group will produce roughly equal results, as compared with other groups. This is not going to happen. Nor will it happen for generations to come unless a new and special effort is made. There are two reasons. First, the racist virus in the American blood stream still afflicts us: Negroes will encounter serious personal prejudice for at least another generation. Second, three centuries of sometimes unimaginable mistreatment have taken their toll on the Negro people."[7]

I've learned that white guilt often can be just as powerful—and dangerous—as white racism. That white guilt manifested itself partly in the form of ill-conceived War on Poverty programs. In his closing line of the report's introduction to drive home his point, Moynihan quotes a line from Karl Gunnar Myrdal's book *An American Dilemma: The Negro Problem and Modern Democracy.* Myrdal said: "America is free to choose whether the Negro shall remain her liability or become her opportunity."[8]

That line pretty much sums up the ostentatious thinking that converts white guilt into progressive socialism. To that, I say: bovine excrement! You are not "free to choose" how to leverage a race of people for your political agenda. You can't just simply write off the crime of slavery and the ensuing discriminatory practices with some poorly thought-out programs just to clear your conscious.

The inhumane treatment of blacks in this country is seared into American history; it will forever be a scar that can't fade away. No amount of make-up—reparations or entitlement programs—will hide its ugly appearance, nor should it.

I can't understand why progressive socialist blacks would allow themselves to be used as political pawns just so white America no longer has to look at its horrific scar in history's mirror. That liability of guilt is white America's battle to fight; knowing that they're wrestling with it is the best penance you'll get, short of turning the tables, enslaving white America for 250 years, and strapping them with crippling, discriminatory laws.

The white guilt and sister feelings of sadness, horror, and embarrassment are normal and rationale emotions given America's history with slavery and systemic racism. It's helpful to understand the levels of this guilt and the nuances of how it is manifested in the form of policies and other action items.

There are white people who directly descend from the early settlers in the 1600s and 1700s who were responsible for wiping out Native Americans and stealing bodies from Africa to become slaves. Katrina Brown, for example, worked with her family to make a DVD called

Traces of the Trade, which tells the story of the De Wolfs, who were the largest slave trading family in early America.[9] The film follows ten descendants of the De Wolf family as they retrace the steps of the triangle trade, visiting the family home in Bristol, Rhode Island, the slave forts in Ghana, and the family plantations in Cuba. The family members honestly grapple with their ancestors' involvement in this horrible enterprise. They genuinely struggle with the issues of white privilege that they experience on their journey. They express genuine remorse.

Then there are the whites who recognize that, yes, their ancestors may have been involved in enslavement of Africans, but those were their great-grandparents' sins and their penance should not be passed down to other generations. They themselves didn't personally consent to slavery and don't feel any obligation to do anything today. In fact, they may even see themselves as victims for being accused of being racists.[10]

And of course, you still have a dwindling minority of white people who participate in white supremacy groups and harbor anger and resentment for how the country has evolved.

The white people who migrated here after the Civil War can claim a level of innocence but may still feel guilty knowing that the opportunities available to them as white immigrants were not open to newly freed slaves.

In his memo about the report to President Johnson, Moynihan tried to leverage another form of white guilt that stems from participating in and benefiting from an immoral system. Moynihan reminded the president that though he was born poor, he still had the advantages not available to blacks. There are people who believe they've benefitted from white privilege and cannot help measuring their lives against the pain and deprivation that black people experienced.[11]

How a politician chooses to mentally grapple with the country's racist past largely determines their stance on the socioeconomic disparities between blacks and whites.

Sorry; it's not my intent to lead you down a psychological rabbit hole to define guilt, but this is all relevant and fits within the context of our discussion of why some push for equality of opportunity and others push for equality of outcomes. We started this discussion on white guilt by affirming that it is normal, though nuanced depending on the person. A healthy response to this uneasy white guilt seeks to keep America focused on ending racism. It seeks to treat every person with dignity and respect. It's about making brave, small steps to ensure everyone has an opportunity to succeed.

Conversely, a negative response to white guilt leads to an assumption that enough race-based policies and targeted handouts to blacks will eventually settle the score and finally wash all hands of any lingering guilt.

When black people recognize the sources of these policy initiatives, they can more intelligently pull back the veil on their attractive freebies. Everything has a price tag attached to it. Nothing in life is free.

So, the problem is not necessarily with Moynihan's diagnosis of socioeconomic disparities or even his desire to fix it; the problem lies in his prescription. A brief closing section of his report with the heading "The Case for National Action" indicates that Moynihan expected strong federal responses. In boldface, he concluded: "The policy of the United States [should be] to bring the Negro American to full and equal sharing in the responsibilities and rewards of citizenship. To this end, the programs of the Federal government bearing on this objective shall be designed to have the effect, directly or indirectly, of enhancing the stability and resources of the Negro American family."[12]

However, as noted black American economist Thomas Sowell wrote in 1993, "Much of the social history of the Western world over the past three decades has involved replacing what worked with what sounded good. In area after area—crime, education, housing, race relations—the situation has gotten worse after the bright new theories were put into operation."[13] To Lyndon B. Johnson's advisors, it sounded like a good idea to do something about the disparities between black and white American families that Moynihan's report revealed.[14] But the sweeping solutions President Johnson's administration chose to enact afterward were no real solutions at all.

Shortly after Moynihan's report was printed, President Johnson invited Moynihan to help him write a speech to be delivered at the graduation ceremonies of Howard University in early June. There, he told the graduating black students and their families: "You do not take a person who, for years, has been hobbled by chains and liberate him, bring him up to the starting line of a race and then say, 'You are free to compete with all the others,' and still justly believe that you have been completely fair. Thus, it is not enough just to open the gates of opportunity. All our citizens must have the ability to walk through those gates."[15]

The major pillars of the Great Society's War on Poverty were the Economic Opportunity Act of 1964, the Food Stamp Act of 1964, the Elementary and Secondary Education Act of 1965, and the Social Security Act of 1965. Underneath these laws were several costly social welfare programs, including money for the poor, from rural Appalachia to inner-city ghettos.

The Economic Opportunity Act in particular made way for Job Corps, Volunteers in Service to America (VISTA), Upward Bound, Head Start, Legal Services, the Neighborhood Youth Corps, the Community Action Program (CAP), the college work-study program, neighborhood development centers, small-business loan programs, rural programs, migrant worker programs, remedial education projects, and local health-care centers.

According to Charles Butler, member of the Project 21 National Advisory Council, "President Johnson's War on Poverty . . . is perhaps the only government institution that destroyed and devastated the black American upward mobility and family structure. As an assistant secretary of labor, Daniel Patrick Moynihan warned that the premise and concept of the War on Poverty would be detrimental to black America. The infamous split between the races that Moynihan predicted has created a deficit between white and black in key areas such as education, income and net worth."[16]

The gap between the expansive intentions of the War on Poverty and its relatively modest achievements fueled later conservative arguments that government is not an appropriate vehicle for solving social problems.[17] After all, that's one of the main differences between conservatives and progressive socialists. As conservatives, we believe in having less government and equality of opportunities; progressive socialists, on the other hand, believe in bigger government and equality of outcomes. Clearly, the War on Poverty proved conservatives right—yet again. The government has never been successful in carrying out the task of personal uplifting. You can't throw money at a problem of people being unwilling to better themselves.

Handouts are popular with people, and they are a surefire way of getting elected. That's why, throughout 1964 and 1965, President Johnson's approval ratings hovered around 70 percent, which clearly explains why he won the 1964 election in a historic landslide.[18] During those same two years, Johnson surpassed all twentieth-century presidents—including Franklin D. Roosevelt—in the number of important progressive programs he managed to steer through Congress.[19] But handouts are also a surefire way of becoming economically enslaved because now we depend on the gubmint for that regular check. We depend on it as it were manna from Heaven. But it's not. It's the plague!

Even though Johnson's collapse was as startling as his ascent—his approval ratings fell to 35 percent in 1967 and 1968, especially due to the unanticipated costs of the Great Society program and the opposition to his policy in Vietnam—the terrifying damage to the black community had already been done, and it would have a ripple effect for decades to come.[20] Indeed, Moynihan was right when he wrote that the country was about to face a new crisis in race relations. However, the way Johnson tried to prevent this catastrophe from happening only secured its predicted arrival.

CHAPTER THIRTEEN

PRESIDENT NIXON'S SUPPORT TO INTEGRATE

Richard Nixon made some key political missteps with black voters in his first run for the White House against John F. Kennedy in 1960. Black voters took note of his failure to telephone Coretta Scott King when her husband was unfairly jailed. In a broader sense, the Republican platform was betwixt strategies of how to appeal to both the antiblack white southerners and the new black voters demanding civil rights.

Those missteps aside, when Nixon finally became president in 1969, he actually made important headway in advancing the socioeconomic status of black Americans. His work to fully integrate schools and support black-owned businesses is often overlooked by civil rights historians.

Elements of his inaugural speech on January 20, 1969, set the tone for how he would lead: "No man can be fully free while his neighbor is not. To go forward at all is to go forward together. This means black and white together, as one nation, not two. The laws have caught up with our conscience. What remains is to give life to what is in the law: to insure at last that as all are born equal in dignity before God, all are born equal in dignity before man."[1]

Despite the unanimous ruling in *Brown v. Board of Education of Topeka* (1954) and the passage of the 1964 Civil Rights Bill, 80 percent of schools remained segregated throughout the nation's South.[2]

In 1969, in another unanimous decision, the Supreme Court decided in *Alexander v. Holmes County Board of Education* "to terminate dual school systems at once and to operate now and hereafter unitary schools."

The Nixon administration chose to adopt the policy position of a unitary school system. They avoided the controversial issue of busing by requiring children, regardless of race, to attend the schools closest to their homes.[3]

In early 1970, Nixon formed a cabinet committee to solve the impasse. The administration's position was to enforce the *Brown* decision that integration "should take place with all deliberate speed," but rather than the federal government forcing how the matter would be resolved, it would be left up to biracial committees representing each of the seven southern states.[4]

The plan proved pivotal to the end of school segregation. In fall 1969, six hundred thousand blacks attended desegregated schools in the South; one year later, three million had been integrated. In 1968, nearly 70 percent of black children were segregated from their white peers; by the end of Nixon's first term, it was just 8 percent.[5]

Nixon's record in promoting black businesses is also noteworthy. Following conservative principles, he didn't impose rules on private enterprises to hire black contractors. Instead, he led by example. The Nixon administration worked to end discrimination in companies and labor unions that received federal contracts. The policy—which called for hiring certain percentages of black and female employees—initially included government contracts in excess of $500,000 in the construction trade and later expanded to include contracts of $50,000 or more in all areas of industry.[6]

President Nixon also signed the Equal Employment Opportunity Act of 1972, which gave the government more power to fight workplace discrimination. Between 1969 and 1972, the EEOC staff had increased from 359 to 1,640, and its budget increased from $13.2 million to $29 million.[7] Note that this was not a handout to any particular minority group; rather, it was money spent to enforce an equal opportunity for success for those minorities who chose to work. That's a key distinction.

Under the Nixon administration, government assistance to black-owned business enterprises more than doubled. Federal purchases increased from $13 million to $142 million from 1969 to 1971, and total revenues from black businesses jumped from $4.5 billion in 1968 to $7.26 billion in 1972. By 1974, two-thirds of the one hundred largest black enterprises had been started during the Nixon administration.[8] You see, the main difference between what Johnson did and what Nixon did is this: Johnson gave handouts to the black community, thus creating a system of economic enslavement; Nixon instead helped black people become economically independent by financially helping them create and set up businesses. At the end of the day, black business owners were able to go home feeling accomplished and proud in their ability to provide for their family, not to mention they now had the opportunity to save money and eventually become homeowners as well—just like my parents did. Instead, black people during Johnson's administration sat down and waited for that next gubmint check to come, depending on it.

Clearly, President Nixon proved that, even in modern times, the Republican Party, living by its conservative values, has the best interests of black America at heart.

CHAPTER FOURTEEN

PRESIDENT CARTER AND THE COMMUNITY REINVESTMENT ACT

In December 1973, Nixon's vice president, Gerald Ford Jr., became the first person appointed to the vice presidency under the terms of the Twenty-Fifth Amendment after the resignation of Spiro Agnew. Ford, a Michigan congressman, joined the Nixon administration while it was in the middle of an impeachment process from the Watergate scandal.

President Nixon's downfall from the Watergate scandal was historic. His impeachment not only overshadowed his work to promote civil rights but hurt the Republican Party's standing in the minds of voters.

That gave the new president, Ford, the dubious honor of being the only person to have served as both vice president and president without being elected to either office by the United States Electoral College. To date, his 895-day presidency was the shortest in US history for a president who did not die in office.

Georgia's Democratic governor, Jimmy Carter, brought a folksy charm to the 1976 election. Voters made a statement that they were ready for change when they elected Carter as the thirty-ninth president. Like his predecessors Ford, Nixon, Johnson, and Kennedy, Carter had also served in the US Navy, as a lieutenant and as a midshipman during World War II. However, his narrative as a southern peanut farmer with a heart for the poor was a welcome change from his predecessors.

The Carter administration's centerpiece legislation was its biggest mistake. The Community Reinvestment Act of 1977 addressed how banking institutions meet the credit needs of the areas they serve, particularly in low- and moderate-income neighborhoods. The law set up a system where federal regulators issue credits, or points, to banks that engage in certain activities to promote growth in poorer communities. Qualifying growth actions include giving loans to businesses, community investments, and poor consumers looking to buy a home in designated areas. Those credits are then used to issue each bank a performance rating. The law requires these ratings to be taken into account when banks apply for charters, branches, or mergers and acquisitions, among other things.

Here's the problem. By encouraging lending in poorer neighborhoods, the Community Reinvestment Act also encouraged the issuance of higher-risk loans to borrowers likely to have repayment problems. Banks were incentivized to issue high-interest loans. The incentive was so strong that many reports surfaced later indicating that black homeowners who otherwise would have qualified for lower-interest loans were steered toward higher-interest loans to ultimately give the bank a higher rating under the law, thus negatively affecting black families' finances. And what happens once their economic status starts crumbling down? It has a ripple effect into many other aspects of their lives, affecting their businesses, their ability to pay bills, their family life, and more.

When the mortgage meltdown and recession occurred in 2007 through 2009, those black homeowners were impacted the most by foreclosures. Ironically, the very law that was supposed to put black people in homes was now impeding economic recovery because the law couldn't generate enough incentives to increase credit availability to qualified low- to moderate-income borrowers.[1]

In a nutshell, hedge funds and banks created mortgage-backed securities. Insurance companies covered those securities with highly complicated credit default swaps.[2] The demand for mortgages led to an asset bubble in housing. When the Federal Reserve raised the federal funds rate, all those adjustable mortgage interest rates—usually given to lower-income homebuyers taking on more house than they could afford—skyrocketed.[3] That set off a chain reaction. Home prices fell drastically, and low-income borrowers defaulted. Derivatives—financial contracts in which buyers agree to purchase an asset on a specific date at a specific price—spread the risk into every corner of the world. That led to the 2007 banking crisis, the 2008 financial crisis, and the Great Recession.[4]

But like many of the laws passed in Johnson's Great Society platform, the Community Reinvestment Act started with good intentions. Before the law, there was a genuine concern that banks in these poorer neighborhoods were taking deposits from hardworking black residents but weren't allowing them to reinvest those funds to enrich their lives or their communities. The banks, reportedly, were loaning those deposits out to fund other initiatives.

During that time, US banks began to expand their operations across designated geographical boundaries. For example, large regional banks in the 1960s and 1970s expanded their lending operations internationally and, in some cases, established foreign branches. The US banking system was also transitioning from a system characterized primarily by unit banking, in which a small, independent bank operated solely in one state with no branches, to interstate banking.[5]

Another motivation that sparked the Community Reinvestment Act was the desire to discourage redlining practices, meaning a bank would refuse to make credit available to neighborhoods in its immediate locality, including the low- to moderate-income neighborhoods where it was collecting deposits.[6] A second type of redlining is the practice of denying a creditworthy applicant a loan for housing located in a certain neighborhood, even though the applicant may qualify for a similar loan in another neighborhood.[7]

Probusiness Republican legislators had their hand in the mortgage crisis as well. I can assure you, there's enough blame to go around for everyone. However, the Community Reinvestment Act is one of the clearest examples of shortsighted thinking to fix social problems. We have to consider how all of these policy proposals will play out thirty to fifty years from now.

We can't take the same immature approach to creating laws that teenagers take with tattoos of their love interests. If so, we'll be stuck with a permanent, costly reminder of a temporary emotion.

As we've seen in this section of the book, the years between Truman's and Carter's administrations—from 1945 to 1981—are when black people lost sight of which political party truly had their best interests at heart, as they were mesmerized by the promise of a better tomorrow and began accepting handouts from the Democratic Party. Since Kennedy made that phone call to Coretta Scott King, black Americans have been convinced that Democrats are the answer to their many problems. But as Johnson's administration showed us, can these problems really be solved with yet another handout? Can't you see that many of the promises the Democratic Party has made to black America are hollow? They are a façade—a soothing and mesmerizing song created to trick us into believing their rhetoric only because it *appears* shinier than the Republicans'.

My fellow black Americans, aren't you tired of depending on those handouts? Aren't you tired of waiting on the gubmint to tell you who you are, what you are worth, and where you belong? Aren't you tired of being economically enslaved? Come on, we can do better.

We can overcome!

PART III

TWENTY-FIRST CENTURY
ECONOMIC PLANTATION

CHAPTER FIFTEEN

BLACK LIVES MATTER . . . WHICH ONES?

As we've just seen in the previous chapters, in the span of less than forty years, the Democratic Party has gained ground in the black community, establishing itself as the manna from Heaven, the answer to all the problems black America is facing, the only way forward for black people. But if we lift that friendly façade they so carefully crafted in front of the cameras, we will find nothing but a bunch of impostors!

Where were they when the Republican Party was fighting to end slavery? Let us not forget that it was within the core values of the party of Lincoln that the black community found its identity. Could it be just a coincidence that the moment black America became enticed by the empty promises made by progressive socialists was also the moment black families—the heart of the black community—were broken?

Long gone are the days when black men and women owned their own businesses and found pride in working hard to have the ability to feed and sustain their family. Those days have now been replaced with single-parent households who wait on checks from the gubmint. Long gone are the days when black people helped each other learn how to read and write—while hiding from the very people who made up the Democratic Party, may I add—supported each other's businesses, and rallied together to defend their country. These days have now been replaced with an increasing percentage of black-on-black violence, public disrespect for the flag, and unwillingness to learn a trade or get an education.

All because the black community has lost sight of which political party is truly on their side. All because the black community has been duped into believing that they don't know better, that they should wait on progressive socialists to tell them who they are, what they can do, and where they belong. Do you remember what Frederick Douglass's master, Mr. Auld, told his wife when he found out that she was teaching young Douglass how to read and write? He said that an educated slave is forever unfit to be enslaved. And do you know why? Because educated slaves know their own true value and will rebel against a status quo that does not belong to them.

Yet here we are.

Two hundred years later, the black community has become economically enslaved by the same people who pushed to keep them illiterate and physically enslaved when Douglass was alive; the same people who spoke so highly of Dr. Martin Luther King Jr. and the civil rights movement in front of the cameras while, in the background, they were coming up with strategies to prevent him from ever marching on our nation's capital; the same people who decided to start giving out handouts to an entire community to keep them content and at bay instead of empowering them with real support and real solutions.

My question to you, fellow black Americans, is this: Don't you think it's time we started fighting against this twenty-first century economic plantation created by the progressive socialists?

If you are not fully aware of the tragedy that has afflicted the black community since the Democratic Party took over, let me remind you of some of the most crucial events that have affected our people in recent history.

BLACK LIVES MATTER

I know his name.

It was February 1999 when New York City police officers killed Amadou Diallo, a twenty-two-year-old unarmed West African immigrant, just in front of his apartment building in the Bronx borough of New York City.

At around midnight, Diallo arrived at his apartment at 1157 Wheeler Avenue after a long day of working as a street peddler, selling socks, gloves, and videos on Fourteenth Street in Manhattan.[1] When he got home, Diallo chatted briefly with his roommate, Momodou Kujabi, about paying an upcoming electricity bill. Kujabi then went to bed, and Diallo left the apartment to get something to eat, like he did most nights after work.[2]

Four NYPD officers in plain clothes were patrolling Diallo's neighborhood in an unmarked car as part of the NYPD Street Crimes Unit. They were looking for a serial rapist.

Details are unclear about the circumstances of the interaction between Diallo and those four officers—Sean Carroll, thirty-five; Edward McMellon, twenty-six; Kenneth Boss, twenty-seven; and Richard Murphy, twenty-six. The officers, all white and armed with nine-millimeter semiautomatic service pistols, said Diallo ignored verbal commands, and they thought he had a gun. It turned out to be just a wallet.

At 12:44 a.m., as Diallo was trying to get into his apartment, Officers Carroll and McMellon fired all sixteen of their bullets—maximum capacity for their nine-millimeters pistols—at Diallo. Officer Boss fired five shots, and Officer Murphy fired four shots. According to protocol, the officers were told to not fire warning shots. They were instructed to aim for the center of the body—and they did. Of the forty-one shots fired, nineteen landed as intended.

In court, Diallo's attorney argued that he simply may have been reaching for his wallet to hand it over to what he thought was a gang of robbers. Or perhaps he was trying to show the officers his identification.[3] The officers' snap judgment about Diallo when they first saw him from their car and their failure to think through the situation showed a recklessness and complete lack of concern for Diallo's life, according to his attorney.[4]

Diallo—a skinny, shy man from Guinea described as having an easy smile—had been in the United States for two years.[5] He came here seeking a better life.

"We have a very undemocratic society back home, and then we come here. We don't expect to be killed by law enforcement officers," a friend, Demba Sanyang, thirty-nine, told the *New York Times* a day after the shooting.

The four NYPD officers were acquitted of all charges. Protests erupted in the streets.

Deaths like these—mostly of black men—from police mistaking an identity or having a general lapse in judgment have become rallying cries in the black community. These types of killings occurred long before that cold morning in February 1999, and they're still happening today.

Timothy Loehmann, the officer who fatally shot twelve-year-old Tamir Rice in Cleveland, was never criminally charged in the 2014 death. That year also included the deaths of Michael Brown in Ferguson, Missouri; Eric Garner in Staten Island, New York; Akai Gurley in Brooklyn, New York; and Laquan McDonald in Chicago, Illinois.

In 2015, more black deaths at the hands of police were added to the list, including Christian Taylor in Arlington, Texas; Samuel DuBose in Cincinnati, Ohio; Sandra Bland in a Waller County jail cell in Hempstead, Texas; Freddie Gray in Baltimore, Maryland; and Walter L. Scott in North Charleston, South Carolina.

From 2016 to 2018, deaths included Keith Lamont Scott in Charlotte, North Carolina; Paul O'Neal in Chicago, Illinois; Alton B. Sterling in Baton Rouge, Louisiana; Terence Crutcher in Tulsa, Oklahoma; Philando Castile in Falcon Heights, Minnesota; and Botham Shem Jean in Dallas, Texas.

I know their names.

I've chronicled their headlines, and I've prayed for their families.

However, my prayers and concern for the social conditions that led to many of their deaths runs counter to the narrative that progressive socialists try to push. It sickens me how progressive socialists leverage our raw emotions for political gain.

Conservatives shouldn't allow the progressive socialists to corner the market on professing concern over the police shootings of unarmed black men and women. They're crafty at painting conservatives as being insensitive to the killings. And that's why I'm a problem for them; not only do I know the names of the deceased, they are my brothers, sons, and nephews.

To be sure, we conservatives haven't helped ourselves either. We will continue to lose the attention of some minority voters until we come to grips with the fact that we can simultaneously support the brave work of our officers and still be critical of those who overstep their oaths to protect and serve. We can learn their names and still "back the blue."

That false narrative pushed by the progressive socialist left is what gave life to the Black Lives Matter group. By most accounts, Black Lives Matter started in 2013 following the trial of George Zimmerman, who was acquitted of killing an unarmed seventeen-year-old Trayvon Martin in Sanford, Florida, on the grounds of self-defense.

Author and labor organizer Alicia Garza is credited by many with coining the name "Black Lives Matter" in protest.[6] Activist and college professor Patrisse Cullors and Black Alliance for Just Immigration executive director Opal Tometi added fuel to the phrase as a social media hashtag, "#BlackLivesMatter."[7] In 2014, the movement gained significant traction after the fatal shooting of Michael Brown.[8] That was the national tipping point that made the organization a household name.

There are at least two versions of Black Lives Matter. There's the Black Lives Matter network founded by the three black female activists who created the #BlackLivesMatter hashtag. Then there's the Black

Lives Matter movement, a more amorphous collection of racial justice groups.[9]

The Black Lives Matter network is structured and has twenty-four chapters; the Black Lives Matter movement is decentralized and relies "almost solely on local, rather than national, leadership."[10] The movement "eschews hierarchy and centralized leadership."[11] According to one of the Black Lives Matter originating activists, Patrisse Cullors, the movement's "organizing is often spontaneous and not directed by one person or group of people."[12]

From what I gather, the money for the organization comes from progressive socialist groups.[13] In addition, wealthy donors who are household names for Democratic candidates are also funding the movement. Organizations connected with billionaire George Soros are reported to have provided more than $30 million to various Black Lives Matter groups since 2016.[14] It is estimated that since 2013, groups related to Black Lives Matter have taken in $133 million.

It's difficult to pin down the agenda of Black Lives Matter. What started as a targeted response to police killing unarmed blacks has morphed into a broad, unstrategized fight for anyone who feels offended.

An excerpt from their website in the "What We Believe" section:

> We are unapologetically Black in our positioning. In affirming that Black Lives Matter, we need not qualify our position. To love and desire freedom and justice for ourselves is a prerequisite for wanting the same for others.
>
> We see ourselves as part of the global Black family, and we are aware of the different ways we are impacted or privileged as Black people who exist in different parts of the world.
>
> We are guided by the fact that all Black lives matter, regardless of actual or perceived sexual identity, gender identity,

gender expression, economic status, ability, disability, religious beliefs or disbeliefs, immigration status, or location.

We make space for transgender brothers and sisters to participate and lead.

We are self-reflexive and do the work required to dismantle cisgender privilege and uplift Black trans folk, especially Black trans women who continue to be disproportionately impacted by trans-antagonistic violence.

We build a space that affirms Black women and is free from sexism, misogyny, and environments in which men are centered.

This amorphous target and disregard for the Christian faith is why we can't put Black Lives Matter on par with the civil rights movement of the 1950s and 1960s. The proof is in their protests.

When Black Lives Matter groups protest, they assume an aggressive, confrontational disposition. You can't tell the true activists from the mobs who loot and burn stores. It's hard to get an older generation like mine—which has decades of organizational experience—to follow a group with members openly attacking police officers or wearing do-rags, bandanas, and sagging pants. Even if you say that Black Lives Matter activists aren't the people participating in the looting, burning, and violence against police, they still aren't speaking out against that behavior.

By contrast, the peaceful, nonviolent protests and marches of the civil rights movement showed a clear distinction between good and evil. Images circulated across the globe of young black men and women—often times wearing neat church clothes—singing hymns and praying, even in the face of vicious dogs, fire hoses, and police clubs. Their approach was backed by Christian principles. Their targets were focused—let us sit where we want on the bus, pay us fair wages, let us vote, etc. They rehearsed before marching and mimicked the disciplined behavior of their black church leaders.

We have a modern-day example of this attitude that hearkens back to the civil rights era. On June 17, 2015, twenty-one-year-old white supremacist Dylann Roof walked into a prayer service at the Emanuel African Methodist Episcopal Church in downtown Charleston, South Carolina, and he was greeted with love. Not knowing what would soon happen, the twelve church members welcomed him to participate in their Bible study and prayer service. Dylann Roof, wearing a gray sweat-shirt and jeans, stayed there for nearly an hour, listening to the group discuss scriptures.

He waited until they began to pray with bowed heads and closed eyes. He then stood up, removed a Glock 41 .45-caliber handgun from his fanny pack, and aimed it at eighty-seven-year-old Susie Jackson. Her nephew dove in front of Jackson and was shot first. Dylann Roof shouted racial epithets during the six-minute massacre that killed nine people. According to surviving church members, he said, "Y'all want something to pray about? I'll give you something to pray about." Some members survived by pretending to be dead. He had been carrying eight magazines holding hollow-point bullets.

Among the victims were Susie Jackson, eighty-seven; Clementa Pinckney, forty-one; Cynthia Marie Graham Hurd, fifty-four; Ethel Lee Lance, seventy; Depayne Middleton, forty-nine; Tywanza Sanders, twen-ty-six; Daniel Simmons, seventy-four; Sharonda Coleman-Singleton, forty-five; and Myra Thompson, fifty-nine.

I know their names.

He fled the scene and was eventually captured at a traffic stop roughly 245 miles from the shooting scene, driving a black Hyundai Elantra with a three-flag Confederate States of America bumper sticker.

Here's the part that gets me. At the court hearing, when the survivors and the relatives of five of the victims spoke directly to Dylann Roof, they told him they forgave him and that they were praying for God to "have mercy on [his] soul."[15] That's an approach from a different era. It runs counter to the Black Lives Matter movement.

I have a problem with the focus of Black Lives Matter. Making all law enforcement the focal point of your anger is shortsighted, to say the least. The FBI reported that the July 2016 attacks on police in Baton Rouge, Louisiana, and Dallas, Texas, were "influenced by the Black Lives Matter movement."[16] The Dallas attack happened at the end of a Black Lives Matter protest when a gunman who had a vendetta against white cops killed five and injured several other on-duty officers.[17]

Somewhat similar to my complaint about LBJ's War on Poverty and Jimmy Carter's Community Reinvestment Act, we don't consider the impact of our actions thirty to fifty years from now. Let's extrapolate the impact of their widespread targeting of all law enforcement. Already, departments across the country are struggling to find enough applicants for available police jobs.[18]

According to the Bureau of Justice Statistics, about 700,000 full-time sworn officers are working right now in the United States. That's a drop of 23,000 officers since 2013, marking the first big dip since the 1990s.[19] Given that our population is growing, that's a problem. Twenty years ago, there used to be 2.42 officers for every thousand residents; now there are closer to 2.1.[20]

Is the Black Lives Matter movement really prepared for a society with no police officers? That's where we're headed. What young person coming out of high school or college would want to pursue the noble career of law enforcement when all they witness is hatred toward their profession?

The Black Lives Matter activists are incensed when people say "all lives matter" or "blue lives matter" in reference to the police. They say that those slogans take away from the spotlight of black suffering. Instead, they would be wise to remember the words of Martin Luther King: "Injustice anywhere is a threat to justice everywhere."

Black lives matter. OK, but which black lives are we talking about? Are we talking about the black-on-black crime in urban cities like Chicago? At the time of writing this book, just five months into the year, 171 homicides have occurred in Chicago.[21] In the past twelve months, 305 young black men have been killed in Chicago.[22]

So, for the Black Lives Matter activists, here are some names of deaths you don't know, all occurring in Chicago during a seven-day period preceding my writing this very paragraph: Kendrick Woods, twenty-eight years old, male, died at 1:13 a.m. on May 12; Christopher Williams, twenty-three years old, male, died at 11:06 p.m. on May 13; Cartez Brown, twenty-two years old, male, died 3:59 p.m. on May 14; Caleb Springfield, eighteen years old, male, died at 1:59 p.m. on May 14; Jaylin Ellzey, fifteen years old, male, died at 2:16 p.m. on May 14; Dennis Sackmaster, forty-one years old, male, died at 12:24 a.m. on May 15; Terrance Pouncy, twenty-six years old, male, died at 11:46 p.m. on May 15; Lamario Birge, thirty-six years old, male, died at 2:17 a.m. on May 16; Devante Boldon, twenty-five years old, male, died at 12:53 a.m. on May 17; and Donavon Allen, nineteen years old, male, died at 1:10 p.m. on May 18.[23]

I know their names.

Where are the marches for these young men? Where is the evidence showing that police contributed to their killings? Where are the online petitions for getting answers to their deaths? I thought black lives mattered, right?

Shall I continue?

The cumulative number of abortions from 1967 through June of 2018 was 59.4 million, of which an estimated 20.35 million, or 35 percent, were black babies.[24]

Unfortunately, I never got a chance to know their names.

CHAPTER SIXTEEN

THE DECIMATION OF THE TRADITIONAL BLACK FAMILY

One of the fundamental conservative values is the importance of family. The sacred bond that is created, established, and cherished within the nucleus of family has tremendous effects not only on the family members themselves but also on our entire nation. But black American families are suffering. After centuries of being challenged, torn apart, and abused, most of them are now broken. Unfortunately, this status has had a ripple effect on the entire black community.

For example, even though I do hold reckless police officers accountable for the brutal and senseless killings of innocent and unarmed black men, I suspect that if you closely examine those cases, some of these deaths might not have occurred if the victim had had a stronger family nucleus, especially in cases of the black-on-black crime we've seen in urban areas like Chicago.

Social scientists have long drawn a connection between children being born in two-parent households and their economic, educational, and mental health well-being. But you don't need a litany of expert research from overpaid scientists to tell you that having Momma and Daddy in the house can produce better children.

The Apostle Paul says in Colossians 3:19–20 (New King James Version), "Husbands, love your wives and do not be bitter toward them. Children, obey your parents in all things, for this is well pleasing to the Lord." The Bible is filled with admonitions for mothers and fathers working together to build strong families.

By a long shot, more black children are born into single-family households than children of any other race in the country, as reported by the US Census Bureau.[1] Of the 6.1 million black children in the United States, 65 percent live in a single-parent household. In comparison, of the 8.6 million non-Hispanic white children in the United States, just 24 percent were born in a single-parent household.

And if you're curious, of the 7.3 million Hispanic children in the United States, 41 percent were born in single-family households—still more than 20 percentage points less than black children.

What's interesting about Hispanic Americans is they're the fastest growing segment of the population, but they've still maintained a stronger family structure than black families. From 2008 to 2017, the number of Hispanic children in the United States grew 27 percent, compared to a flat growth rate among black children during that same time period.

To be sure, there's a trend toward fewer children being born today. That spike in Hispanic children is taking the country by storm; they will claim the overwhelming population majority in the near future. The number of white children in this country has actually dropped by 6.2 percent.[2]

Based on their stronger family structure, it should be no secret, then, that Hispanic Americans are also climbing the economic ladder much faster than blacks. Among those who grew up lower middle class, 28 percent of Hispanics have advanced to the upper middle class or higher, compared with only 14 percent of blacks, according to a study by Stanford, Harvard, and Census Bureau researchers. In addition, 14 percent of middle-class Hispanic kids made it to the top of the income scale, compared to 7 percent of blacks.[3] According to the study, Hispanics were also more likely to escape poverty, with 45 percent who grew up in the lowest income bracket making it to the middle class or higher. In comparison, only 25 percent of blacks who were born in poverty made it to the status of middle class or higher.[4]

For their study, the Stanford and Harvard researchers looked at the earnings of people born in the late 1970s and early 1980s. They then compared these people's earnings with their parents' income from the mid-1990s to 2000. The study excluded children or parents who were undocumented immigrants.[5]

Poverty rates among black families vary based on family type. While 23 percent of all black families live below the poverty level, only 8 percent of black families consisting of married couples live in poverty, which is considerably lower than the proportion of black families headed by single women who live below the poverty line—37 percent, according to US Census Bureau data.[6] The highest poverty rates (46 percent) are among black families with children that are headed by single black women.

THE HISTORY OF REMOVING
BLACK MEN FROM THE HOME

The real tragedy is that the current dismal statistics facing the black community haven't improved since Daniel Patrick Moynihan's report to President Johnson in 1965. They've gotten worse.

Earlier, I critiqued the response to Moynihan's report. The advisors went too far in their recommendations for "fixing" the black community. Critique aside, what the report did was shine a spotlight on the state of the black family. The report shouldn't have been a call to action for the government; rather, it should have served as a mirror in which black people could see themselves.

The report served as a warning of where the black community was headed and how it would be increasingly difficult for blacks to reach economic equality if they stayed on their current trajectory. Moynihan was right. The out-of-wedlock birth rate for blacks was 25 percent in 1965,[7] 68 percent in 1991,[8] 72 percent in 2011, and 77 percent in 2015.[9]

For his part, Moynihan attempted to explain to President Johnson and his advisors how black families had become so fatherless. Black families have paid a price for the incredible mistreatment endured over the past three centuries.

Slavery and the prohibitive laws denying equal opportunities that followed have forced black families into a matriarchal structure that is incongruent with the rest of American society. There's nothing more crushing to a family than denying a man the right to care for his family. You strip the black man away from the household, and you've effectively stifled the progress of the people.

That's why slave owners split up black families and worked to keep them from marrying each other. They knew the power of family would threaten their own power structure.

After slavery ended, shouldn't that have fixed the black family? No. War always affects black and white families differently. It is impossible to create a dual personality that will, on one hand, be a fighting man toward the enemy and, on the other, a craven who will accept treatment as less than a man at home.[10]

I know firsthand that there's honor in serving in the military, which underscores a person's right to citizenship. As Frederick Douglass put it, "Once let the black man get upon his person the brass letter, US, let him get an eagle on his button, and a musket on his shoulder and bullets in his pockets, there is no power on earth that can deny that he has earned the right to citizenship." Black war veterans were a threat to the power structure. After being emancipated in 1865, newly freed black men were killed in droves at the hands of supporters of the Confederacy. Decades of lynching and terroristic actions worked in tandem to keep black families apart.

Black men faced the same opposition following World Wars I and II. On July 2, 1946, for example, twenty-one-year-old Medgar Evers, his brother Charles, and four other black World War II veterans went to the courthouse in Decatur, Mississippi, to vote. They had been the first black people to attempt to register to vote there since Reconstruction. The six veterans had returned home after fighting for democracy in France and England to find that they were still only second-class citizens.[11]

When they arrived at the courthouse that Election Day, fifteen to twenty armed white men were waiting for them, so Evers and his friends went home to get their guns. The mob was still waiting when they returned. Both Medgar and his brother—Medgar especially—would go on to become important leaders in Mississippi's freedom movement, providing crucial support to the Student Nonviolent Coordinating Committee.

Langston Hughes summed up this "hero's welcome" such black men encountered:

> Looky here, America
> What you done done—
> Let things drift
> Until the riots come.
>
> Now your policemen
> Let your mobs run free.
> I reckon you don't care
> Nothing about me.
>
> You tell me that hitler
> Is a mighty bad man.
> I guess he took lessons
> From the ku klux klan.
>
> You tell me mussolini's
> Got an evil heart.

Well, it mus-a been in Beaumont
That he had his start—

Cause everything that hitler
And Mussolini do,
Negroes get the same
Treatment from you.

You jim crowed me
Before hitler rose to power—
And you're STILL jim crowing me
Right now, this very hour.

Yet you say we're fighting
For democracy
Then why don't democracy
Include me?

I ask you this question
Cause I want to know
How long I got to fight
BOTH HITLER—AND JIM CROW.

—Langston Hughes, "Beaumont to Detroit: 1943"

PUSHING AWAY FROM THE CHURCH

America played a critical role in breaking up the black family and in keeping it from repairing itself. Knowing that you're broken is an incredible psychological weight to carry. Even scripture is seemingly against you. Specifically, the Apostle Paul says to fathers in 1 Timothy

5:8 (NKJV), "But if anyone does not provide for his own, and especially for those of his household, he has denied the faith and is worse than an unbeliever."

Of course, we Christians know how to access God's love to help us carry that weight, psychologically and physically. The Apostle Paul again says in Romans 8:38–39 (KJV), "For I am persuaded, that neither death, nor life, nor angels, nor principalities, nor things present, nor things to come, nor height, nor depth, nor any other creature, shall be able to separate us from the love of God, which is in Christ Jesus our Lord."

The spiritual body of Jesus Christ—the church—has always been a sanctuary for the downtrodden and oppressed. It's in Christ that man finds his true citizenship, which no one can take away. When society denied us opportunities, black families were always able to lean on the church for strength to persevere.

As a nation, we've drifted further and further away from biblical teachings. It's impacted our society. We all need Jesus, especially people who have been oppressed. It makes no sense to me why we would reject the one resource that has been a constant in our survival during the harshest periods of our history in this country. Thinking back to our previous chapter, it's why the civil rights movement was more of a success than the Black Lives Matter movement, even when facing far greater challenges.

We've pushed away from the church and the conservative values that sustained us and, like Judas Iscariot, have traded them in for a few pieces of silver, which in these latter days come in the form of handouts from progressive socialists.

At 41.6 percent, blacks are more likely to participate in government assistance programs in an average month than any other population group in this country, according to the most recent data from the US Census Bureau.[12] In 2016, blacks made up 25.6 percent of food assistance program beneficiaries and 19.1 percent of the recipients of the Temporary Assistance for Needy Families allowance.[13]

I call it the twenty-first century economic plantation because when you have such a large percentage of blacks dependent on the government handing them a check, sadly, it creates a plantation system. We've been complicit in the attempt to weaken our own families. The elite progressive socialists have become our masters, promising blessings and rationing out benefits—to women who keep their men out of the home.

Wake up. It's about control.

We have reason to hang our heads low, given the embarrassing statistics that have come to define us; however, we must remember what we've overcome. Ironically, I take solace in a statement from Moynihan's report. In the midst of describing the deplorable state of the Negro family, Moynihan wrote these words to President Johnson and all the advisors reading his classified report: "That the Negro American has survived at all is extraordinary—a lesser people might simply have died out, as indeed others have. That the Negro community has not only survived, but in this political generation has entered national affairs as a moderate, humane, and constructive national force is the highest testament to the healing powers of the democratic ideal and the creative vitality of the Negro people."[14]

We have overcome. We can overcome again.

CHAPTER SEVENTEEN

WHERE ARE THE SMALL BUSINESSES?

The new generation of black people has been enticed by progressive socialists who claim to be friends and show their affection by offering handouts. This has resulted in young black people sitting in their homes and waiting on their next handout so they can spend that gifted money on a new pair of fancy shoes, a new fancy car, or new fancy jewelry. Materialism has replaced core values that once used to be cherished by black people.

There was a time when black people used to own successful small businesses. How did they become so successful? By cherishing and living by conservative core values. By doing the Christian thing and helping their brothers and sisters so they wouldn't have to rely on the government. By taking pride in financially supporting their family. By sleeping well at night because they knew that they had done it on their own, from the ground up, with their heads held up high.

The importance of small minority-owned businesses can't be overstated. Minority-owned businesses form a significant portion of the US economy. In 2012, eight million minority-owned businesses contributed $1.38 trillion in revenue and 7.2 million jobs to the economy.[1] Their importance was also emphasized during the recent economic recession, when minority-owned businesses were an important source of business growth. From 2007 to 2012—the five years comprising the economic recession—a net two million minority-owned businesses were created while a net one million businesses not owned by minorities closed.[2] During that time, minorities increased their share of overall business ownership from 22 percent to 29 percent.[3] Further minority-owned businesses represented an additional $335 billion in sales and 1.35 million in employment.[4]

The percentage of businesses owned by minorities is growing faster than those minorities' population. For example, the black population grew 6 percent between 2007 and 2012, but their business ownership increased 34 percent.[5] The Hispanic population increased 17 percent, but their businesses increased 46 percent.

Another way of gauging the increase in entrepreneurship is to look at the metric of population per business. Among nonminorities, there is roughly one business for every eight adults, according to the US Small Business Administration. Historically, the ratio among ethnic minorities has been much larger, but it is getting narrower. For black Americans, the ratio is roughly one business for every eleven people. That's good news.

A STATISTICAL FAILURE

However, be warned. Our thirst for positive economic news about black businesses can give us a false sense of accomplishment. Some financial companies have even made up statistics just to capitalize on this growth by selling their services. In 2018, there was a false statistic circulating online that black-owned businesses had increased by 400 percent. After reporters contacted the company pushing that statistic, they removed the mention of it from their website and promotional materials.

The truth is that minority businesses, especially black-owned businesses, have a much smaller share of revenue and employment than their share of all businesses. The gap between share of businesses and sales/employment is described by economists as disparity. Among all ethnic groups, the worst sales and employment disparity belongs to black American business owners, who have a 13 percent disparity ratio for percent of sales and an 18 percent disparity ratio for percent of employment.[6] In comparison, Hispanic business owners have a 33 percent disparity ratio for percentage of sales and a 34 percent disparity for percent of employment.[7] Asian business owners in the United States have the best disparity ratios among ethnic groups, with their share of sales equaling 83 percent of their share of business and their share of employment equaling 90 percent.

Black business owners are far less likely to be employers than any other ethnic group. Of the nearly two million black-owned businesses in the United States, most have no employees. Only 4.2 percent of black-owned firms have hired employees. In contrast, 22 percent of nonminority businesses have at least one paid employee.

One reason for the disparity relates to the industries in which black business owners choose to work. An average of 60 percent of all black-owned businesses—the highest percentage nationally—are in one of the twenty industries with the lowest sales and employment, such as child daycare, independent art, and self-care professions such as barbering and being beauticians. Put another way, all of that wonderful entrepreneurial spirit is being limited to a handful of weakly producing industries. By contrast, there's statistically little to no representation of black-owned businesses in the twenty industries with the highest sales or employment, such as manufacturing and engineering.

However, even within the industries where blacks are heavily represented, they still only account for a disproportionate fraction of overall sales and employment. In the top ten minority industries, minority-owned businesses still only make twenty-four cents for every dollar in sales that a nonminority-owned business makes on average.[8]

George Jefferson, owner of Jefferson Cleaners from the popular 1970s sitcom *The Jeffersons*, is actually a perfect example to illustrate my point. With 52 percent minority representation, the dry cleaning and laundry services business is one of the most popular industries for minorities. However, minorities like Mr. Jefferson account for only 26 percent of the sales and 24 percent of the employment in that industry, according to the Small Business Administration's data. Essentially, Mr. Jefferson's "deluxe apartment in the sky" should be bigger.

We have to grow beyond the point of creating a business just for the sake of creating a business. Anybody can fill out paperwork, pay the required processing fees, and set up a company. However, it takes fortitude, a steely resolve, and capital to make it thrive.

Historically, the problem with black people has been that they have become addicted to being consumers of wealth instead of producers of wealth. This skewed mind-set was prevalent even back in my day as a youth in Georgia, where everybody had to have a Lincoln or Cadillac like Mr. Charley down the street or a fur coat like his wife. Unfortunately, that mind-set has manifested in today's hip-hop generation, which is suffocating with materialism. Songs and movies glamorize capturing expensive cars and clothes.

One could argue that, for many blacks, setting up a business has been reduced to another "must-have" possession rather than a source of economic stability for the family, like it should be. The statistics clearly show that we have the ability to start businesses, but the statistics also show that we're lacking something needed to keep them going.

PROUD BUSINESS HISTORY

We used to have thriving black business districts in an era when it was even more difficult to succeed than it is today. Growing up in Atlanta, I remember traveling up and down Auburn Avenue and seeing successful businesses and social organizations. One of the many impressive buildings was the Atlanta Life Insurance Company, the second-largest black insurance company in the United States, founded in 1905 by former slave Alonzo Herndon.[9] The district also included the Rucker Building, Atlanta's first black-owned office building, built in 1904 by businessman Henry A. Rucker.[10] We even had a thriving black-owned newspaper along the street, the *Atlanta Daily World*, which was founded in 1928.

But "Sweet Auburn," as it was affectionately dubbed by John Wesley Dobbs, fell victim to the same issues as other prominent black business districts nationwide. Lack of investment, crime, abandonment, and highway construction ripped the community apart.

Similarly, neighborhoods in Houston, Texas, had strong black business districts from the 1920s through the 1950s. Black business owners there were known for appealing to racial solidarity and pride as well as the idea of self-help within the black community.[11] In particular, Houston's Fifth Ward, one of the city's six political districts, became a mecca for black businesses. Fifth Ward is conveniently positioned next to the Houston Ship Channel and railroad yards, which made it easier for black men to find attractive work. By 1925, more than forty black-owned businesses had been established along Lyons Avenue, a main thoroughfare in Fifth Ward.[12] Phillis Wheatley High School in Fifth Ward gave birth to some of the country's greatest musicians, including Arnett Cobb, Illinois Jacquet, Lester Williams, and Joe Sample, the jazz piano player.

But like Auburn Avenue, over the last fifty years Fifth Ward has been riddled with crime, drugs, and a lack of investments. The descent started in the 1960s, with musicians like Weldon "Juke Boy" Bonner warning people to "stay off Lyons Avenue," and extended through the 1990s, with rappers detailing the violence and drug scene of Fifth Ward in their lyrics.[13]

Today, Fifth Ward's black business class has been replaced through Latin American immigration. Latino students make up 38 percent of the student body at Wheatley High School, and 40 percent of the population of modern Fifth Ward is Latino.[14]

Of course, the best historical example of black wealth comes from Tulsa, Oklahoma, home of Black Wall Street, where hundreds of successful black-owned businesses lined Greenwood Avenue.

The magic and success of Black Wall Street stems from an effort that flipped racism on its head. In the early 1900s, Tulsa experienced an oil boom, much like Texas, its neighbor to the south. Many blacks came to the area to profit from oil, but they were struck down by harsh Jim Crow laws that left them segregated to the northern part of town. That segregation created the area historians would later dub Black Wall Street.

The town was created in 1906 by entrepreneur O. W. Gurley.[15] By 1921, there were more than eleven thousand residents and hundreds of businesses operated by blacks and patronized by both whites and blacks.[16] Lola T. Williams owned the Dreamland Theatre, which seated nearly one thousand guests for films and live musicals.[17] Close by on Greenwood Avenue was J. B. Stradford's hotel, the largest and most successful black-owned hotel at the time. Stradford bought large tracts of land and sold them exclusively to blacks because he believed that the best way for blacks to reach economic success was to pool their resources together.[18]

Auburn Avenue in Atlanta, Fifth Ward in Houston, and Black Wall Street in Tulsa all succeeded because there was a general consensus among the black business leaders that they could depend on no one but themselves. They created their own access to capital and provided their own business-incubator structure.

Unfortunately, Black Wall Street was the stage of one of the most horrendous and devastating riots in the history of the United States of America. It all began May 30, 1921, when nineteen-year-old Dick Rowland, who worked as a shoe shiner on Main Street, was accused of sexually assaulting a white girl, seventeen-year-old Sarah Page, who worked as an elevator operator in a nearby building. According to her, the assault took place in that very elevator when Rowland rode it to reach the restroom in the building.

Even though nobody knew exactly what had happened, news of the alleged assault spread fast. Two days later, Black Wall Street was on fire. Before the street had even woken up, armed and angry white men destroyed businesses and ransacked homes. Black people—many of whom had served in World War I—tried to defend themselves by fighting back, but the angry mob was backed by the authorities, who had even dispatched airplanes used in World War I to drop firebombs on black residents.

Three hundred black men, women, and children died. Many more were injured and left homeless. Some were even placed in internment camps by the authorities. Indeed, this was one of the deadliest and bloodiest riots in the history of our country.

And yet, not long after, black people returned to Greenwood Avenue and reopened more than two hundred businesses. And they did it without any help from the government. Now *that* is black pride!

Where is that pride now? I believe that the inability of the previously mentioned areas to return to their former glory is an indication that the new generation of black people there has not adhered to the conservative principles that made their forefathers so successful.

WHAT BLACKS CAN LEARN FROM OTHERS

The statistics show that black people aren't as likely to partner with others to help their businesses grow. Minority firms in general are more likely to be owned by one person instead of by a family or more than one business partner.[19] However, within the ethnic minorities, blacks are the greater isolationists in terms of business. We don't share wealth. Asian-owned firms are far more likely to have multiple owners; almost one-fifth (19 percent) of Asian-owned businesses are family owned, compared to 9 percent for black-owned businesses. If you're wondering, 13 percent of Hispanic businesses are owned by multiple family members.

This clearly explains why many of their businesses do so much better than black businesses. Regardless of minority status, firms with multiple owners earn about five times more revenue and employ almost five times more workers than a single-owner firm.[20]

It's sad how the same tactics slave owners used to keep us separate are being perpetuated by us today. We've become the theoretical crabs in a bucket, more interested in keeping each other from climbing out ahead.

That mind-set makes it infinitely more challenging to get access to capital. In many cases, taking on smart business debt is a requirement for growth of a small business. Unless you are able to get a substantial loan, you're not going to have the resources needed to get your business over the hump so it can thrive.

My advice is that when you come across someone who has built a better mousetrap, it's a good idea to observe how they did it. Black America would be smart to look at how the Asian small-business community has been so successful here. When you research their business practices, you'll find how similar they are to those communities in Auburn Avenue, Fifth Ward, and Black Wall Street.

Since the arrival of new immigrants to the United States in 1965, Asian Americans more than any other ethnic group have figured out how to leverage small businesses to provide economic security.[21] One reason they started businesses is because of discrimination in the labor market. As new immigrants, their English wasn't as fluent, their occupational credentials from their home countries often weren't validated by US companies, and they faced discrimination from employers based on their race.

So what did they do? They did what the black men and women of Tulsa did when they faced Jim Crow laws: started their own businesses.

Asian Americans have perfected the ability to set up informal savings and loan arrangements with friends and relatives to get necessary startup capital.[22] According to a 2016 report from the Ewing Marion Kauffman Foundation, 73 percent of Asian-owned businesses used personal and family savings for startup capital.[23] The same study, which also included Census Bureau data, said that black entrepreneurs led all other ethnic groups in relying on personal credit cards to fund new companies or acquire existing companies. The study also found that black entrepreneurs were almost three times more likely than whites to have profits negatively impacted by access to capital.[24]

In addition to relying on family for capital, Asian entrepreneurs lean on their own families and relatives for unpaid or cheap labor. It's also common for them to develop a network of loyal customers within their own ethnic group.[25]

Another theory explaining the success of Asian American entrepreneurs harkens back to lessons from my conservative mentor, Booker T. Washington. Asian immigrants plan from the get-go to open their own businesses using specific education and job skills gained solely for that purpose.[26] For them, starting a business is a not a plan B. It's the only option.

So if Asian immigrants can follow Washington's conservative values to prosperity, why can't we?

CHAPTER EIGHTEEN

SEPARATE AND UNEQUAL: EDUCATION IN AMERICA

Progressive socialism has led us down a path of bondage on a new twenty-first-century plantation. We have allowed the federal government to have greater control over the educational system, which has indirectly worked in tandem with institutional racism to keep our black children behind other races.

The 1954 US Supreme Court case *Brown v. Board of Education* focused on the impact of a legal separation. The court decided that public education was "a right which must be made available to all on equal terms." The federal government would no longer allow states and municipalities to deny equal educational opportunities to a historically oppressed racial minority.[1]

However, in the decades following that historic court case, progressive socialists have worked to give the federal government more control over the educational system. Now, sixty-five years after the landmark *Brown v. Board of Education* ruling, our schools are still separate and still unequal. Almost 40 percent of black and Hispanic students attend schools where more than 90 percent of students are nonwhite.[2] The average white student attends a school where 77 percent of their peers are also white. Schools today are as segregated as they were in the 1960s before busing began.[3]

It's a fact that black students are often concentrated in schools with fewer resources. Schools with 90 percent or more black students spend $733 less per student per year than schools with 90 percent or more white students.[4] In the past, wealthier, predominately white public-school districts would explain away the disparity as simply differences in the property tax bases from which school districts get their funding. However, approximately 40 percent of the variation in per-pupil spending occurs within school districts.[5]

Variation within a district is largely due to district budgeting policies that ignore how much money teachers actually earn.[6] When veteran teachers elect to move to low-need schools in richer, whiter neighborhoods, they bring higher salaries to those schools.[7] New teachers, who tend to start out in high-need schools serving many students of color and poor students, earn comparatively low salaries.[8] This leads to significantly lower per-pupil spending in the schools with the highest concentrations of nonwhite students. It's simple: better teachers produce better students.

If you haven't noticed, I'm passionate about education. Our ability to remain competitive in this new global economy hinges on our ability to properly educate our young people. That's why, when I retired from the United States Army back in 2004, I became a high school teacher in South Florida as part of the Troops to Teachers program. I had a bachelor's and two master's degrees, and my annual pay was $37,000. But I had life experiences that enabled me to make teaching history real, and I was still serving my country.

The History of Separate but Equal

Let's take a step back and figure out how we got here. The Thirteenth Amendment was ratified on December 6, 1865, legally setting free some four million slaves of African descent from fifteen border and Southern states. Ratification took nearly a year; President Abraham Lincoln signed the law on February 1, 1865, but would not live to see it ratified because he was murdered two months later.

Shortly after ratification, Congress passed two more amendments to protect the status of the newly freed slaves. The Fourteenth Amendment provided citizenship, and the Fifteenth Amendment provided the right to vote.

But much of the work Congress did was undercut swiftly by a series of court decisions. Take five-year-old Sara Roberts, for example. She was forced to walk past several white schools to reach the colored primary school.[9] Her father, black printer Benjamin Roberts, filed a lawsuit against the City of Boston to integrate public schools. In 1849, reformer and future US senator Charles Sumner represented Roberts and challenged school segregation in the Boston court.[10] Separate schools for African Americans, he argued, in effect branded "a whole race with the stigma of inferiority and degradation." The Massachusetts Supreme Court, however, upheld segregation in a widely cited ruling.[11] Influential chief justice Lemuel Shaw noted that Boston's separate schools possessed substantially equal facilities and declared that school integration would only increase racial prejudice.

In 1896, the US Supreme Court sanctioned legal separation of the races by its ruling in *Plessy v. Ferguson*, which held that separate but equal facilities did not violate the US Constitution's Fourteenth Amendment.[12]

Beginning in 1909, the newly formed NAACP worked to eliminate racial discrimination and segregation from American life. By the middle of the twentieth century, their focus was on legal challenges to public-school segregation.

The NAACP—back when it was fulfilling its mission—led a direct assault on *Plessy v. Ferguson* and the so-called separate-but-equal doctrine. On May 17, 1954, US Supreme Court justice Earl Warren delivered a unanimous ruling in the civil rights case *Brown v. Board of Education of Topeka* stating that racial segregation of children in public schools was unconstitutional.

It's difficult to appreciate *Brown v. Board* if you don't empathize with the struggle for quality in education before the ruling. I feel that the incredible sacrifices Americans made to educate our forefathers are lost on today's black youth. Perhaps they would respect their opportunities more if they knew about people like Margaret Douglass, a teacher from

Norfolk, Virginia, who was arrested and imprisoned when authorities found out she was teaching free colored children how to read and write from the Bible. According to the 1847 Virginia Criminal Code, "Any white person who shall assemble with slaves, or free negroes . . . for the purpose of instructing them to read or right . . . shall be punished by confinement in the jail . . . and by fine."

More than sixty-five years after that landmark Supreme Court ruling, you would think that our system for educating American youth (regardless of race) would be further along. It's not.

We still have found ways to hold back education from those who need it most. No, we're not arresting people for teaching black children how to read and write, but we've complicated the system and eliminated options for them to be trained by the best teachers.

CARTER ADMINISTRATION'S DEAL WITH TEACHERS UNIONS

We can really place much of the blame on the Carter administration. We've already discussed his impact on the federal housing crisis, but his influence on our educational system is equally appalling.

When Carter was running for president in 1976, his campaign promised the National Education Association he would form the Department of Education.[13] Based on that promise, in 1976 the NEA gave its first presidential endorsement ever, according to the *Washington Post*.[14] During the Democratic National Convention that year, 180 delegates were from the NEA—more than from any other group of any kind.[15] They endorsed Carter and were a major force in getting delegates to the Iowa caucuses.[16]

So is it fair to say that the Department of Education is a creature of the NEA?

"That's true," said NEA executive director Terry Herndon in a 1980 *Washington Post* interview.[17] "There'd be no department without the NEA."

When it was time to pass the bill that created the Department of Education, President Carter's approval rating was below 30 percent.[18] Georgia State University later did a study on the creation of the Department of Education and found that although the department "was fairly low on the list of priorities," President Carter's "Domestic Policy staff did its research, sent people to testify on behalf of the department in Congress, and hoped that their endorsement of the Department would ensure the backing of the NEA and its members for the 1980 election."[19]

Even congressional Democrats weren't fond of the cabinet-level appointment of the education department, according to a report in the Cato Institute's Handbook for Congress.[20]

The teachers unions have arguably hurt the education of our black children by seeking to protect the interests of teachers at any cost. Just do a quick search of recent news on teachers unions nationwide, and you'll find that they mainly work to reduce teacher accountability, shield low-performing teachers from being fired, and push for unsustainable retirement and health benefits.

When it comes to teachers unions, conservatives favor putting students' needs first and ending the union-dominated culture that has prevented educational reforms in public education.[21] Whenever teachers strike for extra pay or to prevent accountability, children suffer.

In 2012, the Chicago Teachers Union went on strike over pay and accountability.[22] As they forced the cancellation of classes for hundreds of thousands of students—leaving families in a bind—they took to the streets carrying signs about how the strike was for the sake of the kids.[23] As seen in that strike and others like it, unions are skilled at using children as pawns in a chess match; it's an unbelievable amount of leverage.

Conservatives support ending the union-dominated contracts that oppose merit pay and advancement and place longevity of teaching over quality of teaching.[24] Conservatives support a merit-based system for public school teachers, and holding teachers accountable has been one of the most difficult things to do.[25] Education has become one of the few fields where a lack of results has no consequences and length of teaching is of greater importance than quality of teaching.

The Carter administration's decision to make the Department of Education a cabinet-level position with more power represents an intrusion by the federal government into an aspect of American society for which there is no constitutional authority.[26] Those brave men that drafted our constitution intended that most aspects of American life would be outside the purview of the federal government. They never envisioned that Congress or the president would become involved in funding schools or mandating policy for classrooms.[27] In fact, in the original constitution, the word "education" is never mentioned. Since 1787, the people have never given the federal government any power over the subject.[28]

American taxpayers have spent billions of dollars on the Department of Education since its founding in 1979, yet test scores and other measures indicate no improvement in American education.[29] In the 1860s, a budget of $15,000 and 4 employees handled education fact finding. By 1965, the Office of Education had more than 2,100 employees and a budget of $1.5 billion. In 2010, the department had nearly 4,300 employees and a budget of about $60 billion. As of fiscal year 2017, the most recent data available, the president's budget provided $69.4 billion in discretionary funding and $139.7 billion in new mandatory funding for the Department of Education.[30]

Progressive socialism is a slippery slope, and we're falling fast.

Still Separate, Still Unequal

Once upon a time, there were chains and locks on exterior school doors to prevent black children from entering. Today, the chains are inside the doors, preventing our children in the inner cities from escaping the failing schools supported by the progressive socialist left and their teacher union cronies.

At grade twelve, the white-black achievement gap in reading was larger in 2015 (30 points) than in 1992 (24 points), while the white-Hispanic reading achievement gap in 2015 (20 points) was not measurably different from the gap in 1992.[31]

In 2011–12, 15.4 percent of black public-school students received an out-of-school suspension—a higher percentage than students from any other racial/ethnic group. In contrast, 1.5 percent of Asian students received an out-of-school suspension—a lower percentage than students from any other racial/ethnic group.[32]

In 2014, a greater percentage of undergraduates were female than male across all racial/ethnic groups. The gap between female and male enrollment was widest among black students (62 versus 38 percent).[33]

In 2011–12, about 72 percent of black students received any type of loans, compared with 56 percent of white students, 51 percent of Hispanic, and 38 percent of Asian.[34]

Black students are far less likely than white students to have access to college-ready courses. You can't learn what you haven't been taught. They're at a disadvantage from the start. Nationwide, only 50 percent of high schools offer calculus, and only 63 percent offer physics.[35] Nationwide, 10–25 percent of high schools do not offer more than one of the core courses in the typical sequence of high school math and science education—such as algebra, geometry, biology, and chemistry.[36]

There is even less access for black students. A quarter of the high schools with the highest percentage of black and Latino students do not offer Algebra II; a third of these schools do not offer chemistry. Fewer than half of American Indian and Alaskan Native high school students have access to the full range of math and science courses in their high school.[37]

Even when black students do have access to higher-level programs in math and science—like gifted and talented or advanced placement programs—they're still underrepresented in those courses. Black and Latino students represent 40 percent of enrollment in schools offering gifted and talented education programs but 26 percent of the students enrolled in those programs.[38]

Black and Latino students combined represent 37 percent of high school enrollment but 27 percent of students taking AP courses, 26 percent of students taking AP exams, and 18 percent of students receiving a qualifying score of three or above on one or more AP exams.[39]

Black students are often located in areas with less qualified teachers or where teachers have fewer years of experience and much lower salaries.[40] Nearly one in four districts with two or more high schools reports a teacher salary gap of more than $5,000 between high schools with the highest and the lowest enrollments of black and Latino students.[41]

While most teachers are certified, nearly half a million students nationwide attend schools where 60 percent of teachers or fewer meet all state certification and licensure requirements. Racial disparities are particularly acute in schools where uncertified and unlicensed teachers are concentrated; nearly 7 percent of the nation's black students—totaling more than half a million students—attend schools where 80 percent of teachers or fewer meet these requirements. Black students are more than four times as likely—and Latino students twice as likely—as white students to attend these schools.[42]

Even among those black students who graduate, many of them aren't considered college ready. In fact, 61 percent of ACT-tested black students in the 2015 high school graduating class met none of the four ACT college readiness benchmarks—nearly twice the rate for all students, 31 percent.[43]

EDUCATION VERSUS INDOCTRINATION

Another problem with our education system today is progressive social-ists gaining control over our school boards. I've always said that the most important elected officials in the United States are not the congressmen or presidents; they're the members of the school board. They have great influence over the future of our next generation of Americans. Even here in Texas, we are witnessing more individuals arriving in Texas from left-leaning states, and they aim on taking over local school boards to implement their agenda early on.

Education in America is supposed to be about preparing our future generations to be exceptional, productive citizens, members of our American society. However, for some that just isn't the case. I am specifically addressing the progressive socialist left.

In *The Communist Manifesto*, written by Karl Marx and Friedrich Engels in 1848, one of their ideological planks is state control of ed-ucation. Why? Marx stated, "The education of all children, from the moment that they can get along without a mother's care, shall be in state institutions." It was Vladimir Lenin who said, "Give me four years to teach the children, and the seed I have sown will never be uprooted," and "Give me just one generation of youth, and I'll transform the whole world."

For the progressive socialist left—Marxists—it's not about educa-tion but rather about indoctrination. This is why the leftists in America want no part of school choice, school vouchers, charter schools, or homeschooling. This is why their leftist teachers unions seek to squash any of these means by which alternatives to their state control of education could possibly exist. This is why we have a generation of young people who actually say they prefer socialism over free-market capitalism.

A recent survey from the Victims of Communism showed that an overwhelming majority of millennials couldn't offer a correct definition of socialism. Most young people have no idea of its deadly ties to Karl Marx's ideology and how it gave birth to people like Mao Zedong, Leon Trotsky, Valdimir Lenin, and the Kim and Castro families.

There's room for education, but we better act fast.

During a speech in Baltimore, Maryland, on April 18, 1864, President Lincoln argued that the world never had a good definition of the word *liberty*. "With some, the word liberty may mean for each man to do as he pleases with himself, and the product of his labor; while with others the same word may mean for some men to do as they please with other men, and the product of other men's labor."

Clearly, President Lincoln understood the nature of progressive socialism and how it would give rise to those men who had a perverted definition of liberty and advocated for tyranny instead.

CONSERVATIVE SOLUTIONS

I'm proud of the conservative stance on education that seeks to limit federal control. The federal government is far too active in developing educational policy. Education should be based on cooperation among the state, local government, and parents, with a built-in accountability system to promote quality curriculums.

Individual states are in the best position to make decisions on funding and strategies for improving poorly performing schools. Let the elected state officials have responsibility for creating the policies that best serve their young people. As it stands, federal overseers are too busy throwing darts in the dark for solutions that ultimately perpetuate failed policies.

Too many school principals complain today about having their hands tied behind their backs because of government mandates. They need the freedom to use their management skills to get better results from teachers and hold them accountable when they fall short. They also need the freedom to tie compensation to teacher performance.

I know my old-school logic may run counter to today's elitist, self-entitled culture, but we need more practical teacher training and less obscure theoretical nonsense that fails to prepare our students for the world.

Given today's global landscape, education is a national security issue. However, poor school performance should be addressed first by giving local officials time to implement their own turnaround plans. If they aren't able or if their plans fail, then we can seek alternative measures. We conservatives have been consistent in this approach.[44]

We must figure out a way to put black parents back in the driver's seat of their child's education while still giving local lawmakers the oversight to evaluate what the students are learning. As a father of two daughters, I know firsthand how seriously loving parents take their role in overseeing education.

Following Booker T. Washington's principles, I'm all in favor of expanding career and technical schools. I'm also in favor of public magnet schools and charter schools, with additional consideration for private school tax credits and vouchers and online schools.[45]

I say, let's apply free-market principles to education by spurring healthy competition among schools so parents can have options. Parent information is the foundation for choices and better educational outcomes. If a parent knows their local school is underperforming, they will demand change or leave the school.

If conservative principles are applied correctly, we can correct the blunder of Jimmy Carter. I for one believe the plight of education in the black community today to be intentional, just like the destruction of the traditional nuclear black family. In the two-parent black household, quality education was cherished, and high standards were demanded of the child and of the school. I know that from my own life, but that has changed.

Still, I believe we can overcome.

PART IV

THE FUTURE FOR THE
AMERICAN BLACK COMMUNITY

CHAPTER NINETEEN

THE RISE OF BLACK PROGRESSIVE SOCIALISM AND TODAY'S TALENTED TENTH

The educational disparities we just uncovered in the previous chapter are even more pronounced within our own race. Unfortunately, that's the way a rising group of progressive socialist blacks prefer it.

The separation of slaves between the field and house was a psychological strategy the master used to keep us from working together and revolting. Typically, the amount of melanin in a slave's skin was the determining factor in where he or she worked. Darker slaves stayed outside, while lighter slaves stayed inside.

The black elite today has perpetuated those psychological chains. Rather than allowing conservative principles to give all people equal opportunity to better themselves, the black elite has allowed white liberals to shackle their ankles and lead them down a path of progressive socialism. The result: the distance between the blacks outside the house and inside the house is growing. We're more separate today than ever before.

Let's go back to the turning point of our intracultural separation here in America. After slavery, as our country was starting the twentieth century, blacks were at a crossroads of how best to move forward with their newly acquired freedom. Booker T. Washington and W. E. B. Du Bois emerged as two of the most preeminent thought leaders for the race. Both had influence among blacks and wealthy white financiers.

In September 1895, Washington delivered a now famous speech before a predominately white audience at the Cotton States and International Exposition in Atlanta. In the speech, unfairly dubbed the

"Atlanta Compromise" by critics like Du Bois, Washington essentially called on blacks to have an industrial mind-set, to take pride in enterprise and hard work, and to not expect additional help from whites—the same concept that so many successful black people applied in Black Wall Street.

During his speech, he told a parable of a ship lost at sea for many days. When the passengers suddenly found a friendly vessel approaching, they issued a signal for water because they were dying of thirst.

> The answer from the friendly vessel at once came back, "Cast down your bucket where you are." A second time the signal, "Water, water; send us water!" ran up from the distressed vessel, and was answered, "Cast down your bucket where you are." And a third and fourth signal for water was answered, "Cast down your bucket where you are." The captain of the distressed vessel, at last heeding the injunction, cast down his bucket, and it came up full of fresh, sparkling water from the mouth of the Amazon River.
>
> To those of my race who depend on bettering their condition in a foreign land or who underestimate the importance of cultivating friendly relations with the Southern white man, who is their next door neighbor, I would say: "Cast down your bucket where you are"—cast it down in making friends in every manly way of the people of all races by whom we are surrounded. Cast it down in agriculture, mechanics, in commerce, in domestic service, and in the professions. And in this connection it is well to bear in mind that whatever other sins the South may be called to bear, when it comes to business, pure and simple, it is in the South that the Negro is given a man's chance in the commercial world, and in nothing is this Exposition more eloquent than in emphasizing this chance.

Friends, that's conservative speech at its finest. Some black leaders like Du Bois saw it as weakness. But Washington didn't stop there; he went further in his speech, indirectly attacking the black elite of the day: "Our greatest danger is that in the great leap from slavery to freedom we may overlook the fact that the masses of us are to live by the productions of our hands, and fail to keep in mind that we shall prosper in proportion as we learn to dignify and glorify common labor, and put brains and skill into the common occupations of life; shall prosper in proportion as we learn to draw the line between the superficial and the substantial, the ornamental gewgaws of life and the useful."

Next came the most famous lines from his speech: "No race can prosper till it learns that there is as much dignity in tilling a field as in writing a poem. It is at the bottom of life we must begin, and not at the top. Nor should we permit our grievances to overshadow our opportunities."

HISTORY OF THE TALENTED TENTH

In direct response to Washington's Atlanta Exposition speech, Henry Lyman Morehouse—a white man for whom Atlanta's Morehouse College is named—first came up with the idea of the "Talented Tenth" during an April 1896 essay.

> In the discussion concerning Negro education we should not forget the talented tenth man. An ordinary education may an- swer for the nine men of mediocrity; but if this is all we offer the talented tenth man, we make a prodigious mistake. The tenth man, with superior natural endowments, symmetrically trained and highly developed, may become a mightier influence, a greater inspiration to others than all the other nine, or nine times nine like them.

> Industrial education is good for the nine; the common English branches are good for the nine; but that tenth man ought to have the best opportunities for making the most of himself for humanity and God. A mere common education will not disclose their uncommon powers; they need the test of the best. And somewhere, at several central points at least, provision should be made for the higher education of the talented tenth as well as ordinary education for the other nine.[1]

For his part, Du Bois takes the concept of the Talented Tenth even further. In *The Negro Problem*—a collection of seven essays from prominent black writers like Washington, Du Bois, and Paul Laurence Dunbar—Du Bois is adamant that there be a hardline separation among blacks. "The Negro race, like all races, is going to be saved by its exceptional men. The problem of education, then, among Negroes must first of all deal with the Talented Tenth; it is the problem of developing the best of this race that they may guide the Mass away from the contamination and death of the Worst, in their own and other races."

Blacks cannot survive with an industrial mind-set alone, Du Bois said. "But unless he have political rights and righteously guarded civic status, he will still remain the poverty-stricken and ignorant plaything of rascals, that he now is. This all sane men know even if they dare not say it."

Not all men can go to college, but some men must, Du Bois argues. "Every isolated group or nation must have its yeast."[2]

To be sure, Du Bois did acknowledge the importance of teaching blacks to work and having access to industrial schools like Hampton and Washington's Tuskegee Institute. However, he pushed for an elite group of blacks to become teachers of their teachers.

There is truth in what both Washington and Du Bois promoted. Our race needed—and still needs—both the thought leaders in business suits and the rank-and-file workers with dirty hands working in fields and factories. For as much as they took jabs at one another, Washington and Du Bois still had much in common and acknowledged and complimented each other later in life.

COLORISM IN THE BLACK COMMUNITY

The main problem I have with the Talented Tenth concept is that in Du Bois's world, it was not up to the man or woman to determine which side of the equation they would live. Who gets to play the role of kingmaker and place a person in the highly exalted 10 percent of the race, and who determines the fate of the poor souls relegated to the 90 percent? That concept speaks of socialism. It says that no matter how hard you work, your fate has already been determined by someone else. Blacks had just come out of slavery; under Du Bois's logic, 90 percent of blacks should willingly trade a white master for an elite black one. The "yeast," as he called them.

The concept of the Talented Tenth becomes even more egregious when you consider the fact that the ten people Du Bois was actually referring to were all of light complexion.

To really get a handle on his problem with colorism, you need to examine not his arguments with Washington but his debates with Marcus Garvey.

Marcus Mosiah Garvey, a stocky, dark-skinned man from the Caribbean, came to the United States in 1916 to raise funds for a school in Jamaica modeled after Washington's world-renowned Tuskegee Institute. Washington, by this time, was already dead, so Garvey reached out to Du Bois at the New York office of the NAACP.[3] When Garvey arrived at the office, he said he was "unable to tell whether he was in a white office or that of the NAACP."[4] The staff was filled with white and light-skinned people.

In making his literary points in his essay "The Talented Tenth," Du Bois—who himself was biracial—named twenty-one present and past black leaders who he felt embodied the characteristics of the elite 10 percent, and all of them except one were light-skinned and biracial.

This was a time when light-skinned blacks were still using brown paper bags and rulers to bar dark-skinned brethren from churches, jobs, civic groups, historically black colleges, fraternities, sororities, and neighborhoods.[5] The children's rhyme of the day was painfully true: "If you're white, you're right / If you're yellow, you're mellow / If you're brown, stick around / If you're black, get back."

Two years after Garvey's visit to the United States, sociologist Edward Byron Reuter wrote *The Mulatto in the United States*, in which he argued that all of the noteworthy achievements of black people came because of light-skinned biracial blacks.[6] It's a racist ideology of colorism that started with Princeton theologian Samuel Stanhope Smith. In 1787, before members of the American Philosophical Society—some of whom would go on to write the US Constitution that year—Smith praised "domestic servants" for having "advanced far before" the darker and Africanized "field slaves" through "acquiring the agreeable and regular features" of "civilized society": light complexion, straight hair, and thin lips.[7]

In an experience similar to Garvey's, author and civil rights activist James Baldwin says in the 2017 documentary *I Am Not Your Negro* that he rejected membership in the NAACP because of "black class distinctions that repelled a shoeshine boy like me."[8]

I can already hear their question: Colonel West, why are you bringing up colorism in the black community? I do so because philosophies like the Talented Tenth, the colorism it promoted, and the proliferation of its messages among the black elite today are another form of socialism, which dissuades black men and women from believing they can have an equal opportunity at a better life.

You do realize that W. E. B. Du Bois encountered socialist ideas while he was studying in Germany, where he occasionally attended rallies of the German Social Democratic Party? This cofounder of the

NAACP joined the Communist Party USA on October 1, 1961, saying in a letter, "Today I have reached a firm conclusion: Capitalism cannot reform itself; it is doomed to self-destruction . . . Communism—the effort to give all men what they need and to ask of each the best they can contribute—this is the only way of human life. It is a difficult and hard end to reach—it has and will make mistakes, but today it marches triumphantly . . . In the end Communism will triumph. I want to help to bring that day."[9]

It pains me to read how young black people are turning to socialism, thinking that it is a form of antiracism. Bovine excrement! Don't they know that socialists are historically progenocide? Natalie Jeffers, a co-founder of the Black Lives Matter movement in the United Kingdom, told her followers: "Fight racism with solidarity. Fight capitalism with socialism. We must organize—dedicate ourselves to revolutionary politic power." The same backward rhetoric is also being shouted from bullhorns of Black Lives Matter and progressive socialist rallies here in the United States.[10]

Do we need a quick history lesson on how the pioneers of socialism dealt with race? The genocide promoted by socialists was responsible for at least eighty million deaths during the course of the twentieth century.[11] In the *New York Tribune* in 1853, Karl Marx came close to advocating genocide, writing, "The classes and the races, too weak to master the new conditions of life, must give way."[12]

I know that colorism today is not like it was during the time of Washington, Du Bois, and Garvey. It's not even the same as it was when I was a child, when the lighter-skinned children were invited to secret Jack and Jill social gatherings. However, the strategy of black elitists applying socialistic principles to somehow improve the lives of all blacks is still going on today. We've left our first love of conservatism.

Du Bois was mighty proud of his Talented Tenth concept, calling these people the "yeast" of the Negroes. However, he would have been wise to heed the warning of the Apostle Paul in 1 Corinthians 5:6 (KJV): "Your glorying is not good. Know ye not that a little leaven [yeast] leaveneth the whole lump?"

Today, black conservatives—the 90 percent—are denigrated, disparaged, and demeaned by white progressive socialists and their hand-selected Talented Tenth. How interesting when you consider Booker T. Washington as the father of black conservatism and W. E. B. Du Bois as the father of black progressive socialism. In the end, it was Du Bois who renounced his American citizenship. It's interesting how the black intellectual and entertainment elites of today find it fashionable to deride America, harping on political agitation and castigating our nation as racist. I am a proud American black man, a conservative, and not part of the Talented Tenth. And frankly, that is just fine by me.

CHAPTER TWENTY

ECONOMIC RESURGENCE FOR THE BLACK COMMUNITY

We, as black Americans, have the power to overcome. Like James Baldwin once said, "Our crowns have been bought and paid for . . . all we have to do is put them on our heads."

Our future is as bright as we want it to be. But it's clear that we need to make some drastic changes to create an economic resurgence for the black community. Over the past thirty years, the average wealth of white families has grown by 84 percent—three times the rate of growth for the black population. If the past thirty years repeat, the next three decades will see the average wealth of white households increase by more than $18,000 per year while black households will see their wealth increase by about $750 per year.[1]

By 2043—the year in which it is projected that people of color will make up a majority of the US population—the wealth divide between white families and black families will have doubled, on average, from about $500,000 in 2013 to more than $1 million.[2]

If the average wealth of black families continues to grow at the same pace it has over the past three decades, it will take black families 228 years to amass the same amount of wealth white families have today.[3]

Given the statistics, closing the wealth gap doesn't have to be our goal as a race. To put it lightly, whites have had a significant head start through slavery and the ensuing Jim Crow laws. For us to genuinely close the wealth gap, we would have to somehow keep whites from gaining wealth for the next two hundred years while simultaneously fixing our own wealth-generation problems. That type of parity is not realistic in this dimension of time.

No amount of reparations will close that enormous wealth gap. It's as difficult as trying to redirect a blowing wind. So do we just give up? No! When you can't change the wind, you adjust your sails.

We should start by measuring ourselves against ourselves. Find new goals for our communities. Here are some starter questions: Have we made significant economic progress within our race during the last forty, fifty, or sixty years? Are our families stronger than they were forty, fifty, or sixty years ago? Have we reduced crime from the rates we experienced forty, fifty, or sixty years ago? You know the answers to those questions.

So how do we fix our issues?

WE NEED JOBS

Don't underestimate the power of employment to lift a community out of poverty. A man with a job is a force to be reckoned with, for his family, his community, and the world that surrounds him.

Without a job to do, he has an idle mind, the proverbial devil's workshop. Jobs are essential to improving black communities. Increased employment improves educational outcomes for black children and reduces crime. Although there is much that criminologists still do not understand about the dynamics of criminal offending, a growing body of research suggests that low wages, high unemployment, high poverty, and high economic inequality lead to higher crime rates.[4]

Education alone will not fix our problems. Sorry, Team Du Bois! We're better educated today than we were in the 1960s, but the unemployment disparity still remains.[5] Even if blacks somehow caught up with whites educationally, unemployment disparities would not disappear, as blacks are more likely to be unemployed than whites at every educational level.[6] In 2007, for example, before any significant unemployment effects of the Great Recession had been felt, blacks twenty-five years old and older with high school diplomas were about twice as likely to be unemployed as their white peers. Blacks with a bachelor's degree or higher were one and a half times as likely to be unemployed as their white counterparts.[7] These disparities are so large that even if blacks had the same educational attainment profile as whites, most of the unemployment gap would remain.[8]

It's a mistake to think—as many do—that blacks, particularly black men, don't have jobs because they lack soft skills like teamwork, adaptability, problem solving, conflict resolution, and leadership. The truth is that we're bubbling over with soft skills. We're overrepresented in the service sector, which has a relatively high demand for soft skills.[9] However, blacks are underrepresented in the construction industry and slightly underrepresented in the manufacturing industry, both of which depend heavily on hard skills.[10] It appears ol' Booker T. Washington was right after all. Since these industries tend to pay higher wages than the service sector, it would be wise for blacks to increase their rates of employment in these industries.[11]

Elements of Washington's speech at the 1895 International Exposition in Atlanta are still relevant today. We're dying of thirst for jobs. Washington would advise us to cast down our buckets where we are. Remember, Washington said in that speech, "We shall prosper in proportion as we learn to dignify and glorify common labor, and put brains and skill into the common occupations of life."

It's as if we've forgotten our roots or are ashamed of them. One of our richest legacies is in construction. Our forefathers built the pyramids of Egypt, and as early as the 1500s, we were brought to this country as slaves to lay the foundations for New York, Philadelphia, Baltimore, Washington, DC, and practically the entire southeastern territories.[12] You mean to tell me we can't muster up enough skill today to build a few parks, houses, and office buildings in our communities?

We have this mentality that it's either a four-year college or bust. The purpose of any education is to put people in position to earn a living and to protect themselves. When our young black boys and girls are in junior high and high school, we should be preparing them to earn a living. For this reason, I'm encouraged by the increase in vocational and technical education programs I've seen emerging across the country's school districts. We need more public-private partnerships to create programs like this in predominately black schools. If ever we are to rise beyond our current condition, we must put together sustainable options for the 90 percent, because the Talented Tenth has failed us.

WE NEED PUBLIC-PRIVATE PARTNERSHIPS

I believe public-private partnerships are a solid conservative approach to helping improve our black communities. The use of philanthropic incentives will help limit the influence and involvement of the federal government.

Organizations like the Association of Black Foundation Executives work with philanthropic institutions and corporations to help build black economic power. The association represents more than $100 billion in assets under management with member organizations like the Bill & Melinda Gates Foundation, the Ford Foundation, and the W. K. Kellogg Foundation. Their goal is to shift the way philanthropy invests in poor communities that are disproportionate.[13] They focus on creating change rather than simply providing charity.

Public-private partnerships tend to work best when addressing areas in which traditional investment is lacking and the risks are too high for individual actors to undertake alone.[14] However, we must figure out how to create more public-private partnerships effectively. A recent analysis of 1,400 public-private partnerships supported by the US Agency for International Development found that fewer than 10 percent of them lasted as long as five years. Case studies have also shown that these types of partnerships produce widely varying levels of impact.[15]

We Need Enterprise and
Economic Empowerment Zones

I'm in favor of more enterprise zones, where companies can qualify for subsidies to help grow their businesses in depressed areas of a community. If you want businesses to invest in a particular area, offer the right tax incentives to get their attention. It's business.

Most states have their own versions of enterprise zones. Typically, the area has to meet the state's definition of distress or blight. Sometimes it's defined by an area with low income, population decline, or a high rate of vacant buildings.

Every big city has those eyesores. Unfortunately, many of our big cities are being controlled by progressive socialists who are dissuading businesses from building operations in the city. We need strong conservative leadership in the major cities. We need leaders who are well versed in how to use property tax abatements, investment tax credits, job creation tax credits, inventory tax exemptions, low-interest loans, and bond financing to get deals done.

We Need to Reduce Recidivism
in the Black Community

Our nation has the largest incarcerated population in the world.[16] Although the United States has only 5 percent of the world's population, it has 25 percent of the world's inmates.[17] After release, formerly incarcerated men are labeled "ex-cons" for the rest of their lives. With this label, they can't get a job, and if they do, it's not enough to provide a livable wage to support a family. Not surprisingly, unemployment rates can be as high as 70 percent among ex-offenders.[18]

Programs like the Prison Entrepreneurship Program are a start in the right direction. Since 2004, PEP has partnered with some of the nation's top executives and MBA students to transform these ex-offenders into entrepreneurs. During their final months in prison, inmates learn the tenets of business. They're taught money-management skills, like preparing a balance sheet and forecasting. In addition, they learn the all-important soft skills that are critical to keeping an enterprise growing.

The program has an entrepreneurship boot camp to help inmates select feasible business ideas and a reentry program that has impressive recidivism statistics. PEP graduates have a low three-year recidivism rate—7.5 percent compared to the national average of nearly 50 percent.[19] More than 360 businesses have been launched by PEP graduates, including a handful that generate more than $1 million in gross annual revenue.[20]

Without innovative programs like this, an ex-offender is on his own with the nearly impossible task of finding a place to live. Having served your sentence and paid your debt to society, you are free, but you face these daunting realities. What would you do? Without support and skills, how successful would your transition be? Without a job or a home, as many as 50 percent of released parolees become homeless and resort to living "on the streets."[21] Unemployment, homelessness, and incarceration become an inescapable cycle, and with few real options, many men return to a life of crime.

Unfortunately, this tragic cycle is why the majority of ex-offenders will commit new crimes within three years of their release from prison. In fact, the United States Department of Justice reports that ex-offenders commit nearly 70 percent of all crimes.[22]

DON'T LET HISTORY REPEAT ITSELF

If we forsake the responsibility of finding solutions to fix our communities—without dependence on the federal government—then we run the risk of history repeating itself. The case being made for reparations is nothing more than a variation of the Daniel Patrick Moynihan mind-set we discussed earlier in this book. Bleeding-heart liberal policy wonks already have tried giving us entitlement programs through President Lyndon Johnson's War on Poverty, and look where that got us.

If you recall, Moynihan felt more needed to be done to help black Americans reach a socioeconomic status equal to whites. "The Negroes are asking for unequal treatment," Moynihan wrote in a classified executive memo. "More seriously, it may be that without unequal treatment, there is no way for them to achieve anything like equal status in the long run."[23]

Their plan ultimately created a deeper welfare state that has trapped many blacks from escaping. Yet social engineers have not ceased trying to implement "bright new theories" that sound good but have no firm economic basis since Thomas Sowell wrote about their history of failure in 1993. Do you honestly think cutting us a check is going to produce different results?

If we're thirsty for an economic resurgence, we should cast down our buckets where we are. Our future is as bright as we want it to be.

Ultimately, we can have a billion great ideas, but if the family structure is not set—if the traditional nuclear black family remains destroyed by progressive socialist policies—then our plans will crumble.

CONCLUSION

Back in 2012, when I was running for my congressional reelection, I was at a polling location in St. Lucie County when a black woman who recognized me came up and said that I should be "ashamed of myself." She said that my parents would be disappointed in me. Sadly, she was horrifically wrong, as my parents, Buck and Snooks West, raised me first and foremost to think for myself. They also raised me based upon conservative principles and values.

I would like to find that woman and put this book into her hands. Chances are she would not read it, and that is exactly the problem in the black community today—a lack of historical and factual education and understanding. Then again, that is also the greater issue in these United States of America. Our system of education, once esteemed, has been usurped by a program of indoctrination.

When I am asked, "Why are you a black conservative?"—well, this book is the response. The real question in the black community should be, "Why are you *not* a conservative?"

My folks raised me with a firm foundation rooted in our Judeo-Christian faith heritage. It was that faith that has sustained the black community through some dark days. So why would the black community embrace the philosophy of progressive socialism, which is firmly established in secular humanism?

Here in America, the black community fought to ensure that they, too, were endowed with unalienable rights from their Creator: life, liberty, and the pursuit of happiness. How can it be that the black community associates with a political party that, at their 2012 national convention, booed God? Why do black ministers lend their support to a political ideology that would deny them their first liberty, the freedom of religion and the free exercise thereof?

169

I was also raised with a true sense of family and its importance. So why does the black community, which worked so hard during slavery and segregation to preserve our families, support a political ideology that has intentionally decimated the traditional nuclear black family? Progressive socialists will staunchly defend the organization Planned Parenthood, founded by a white supremacist and racist, Margaret Sanger. It is that very same organization that has been instrumental in the murder of eighteen million black babies in their mothers' wombs. The policies of Democratic president Lyndon B. Johnson have left the black community with only 24 percent of our children living in two-parent households.[1] And we continue to support our own genocide and destruction?

Blacks dreamed of individual rights, freedom, and responsibility—our pursuit of happiness. So why do we support a political party that still treats us as slaves, offering reparations? Slavery, segregation, and all those ills emanated from one political party; perhaps they should be writing the checks themselves?

The black community strove to have personal rights, yet we support the philosophy of progressive socialism, which is the very embodiment of collective subjugation. That is not what my parents endured in order to set the conditions for my success and certainly not what I want to leave as a legacy to my two daughters. The choice is clear: victim or victor. As it is written in Joshua 24:15 (New American Standard Version), "Choose for yourselves today whom you will serve." Leftists believe that they can guarantee happiness. In the end, they promise only enduring servitude.

My parents sacrificed so much to ensure that I had a great education. They knew that America offered equality of opportunity, which begins with a quality education. Sadly, blacks have trusted a political party that once locked them out of schools and now locks them inside of failing schools. The left is more focused on appeasing teachers unions than making sure our children, especially our children in the inner cities, enjoy equality of opportunity, since all they offer is an equality of outcomes. And if you have not noticed, those outcomes in the inner city have been apocalyptic.

Blacks have always been an industrious people. My philosophical mentor, Booker T. Washington, founded the Tuskegee Normal and Industrial Institute not just for book learning but to develop entrepreneurial skills and self-reliance. We have evidenced the early pioneers of black entrepreneurship. We spoke of those proud business owners operating in Black Wall Street, Sweet Auburn Avenue, and Fifth Ward. These are people and places that were created and existed under the dire specter of segregation. And our families were stronger under segregation. What happened?

My dad did not give me an allowance; he gave me a lawn mower, and I had my own little grass cutting business and washing cars. The free-market economic system has always been a part of the black community, so what happened? Why does the black community associate itself with a socialist economic philosophy that has exacerbated the issues of poverty, welfare, and the dependency society?

Lastly, as I have articulated, the West family is a family of combat veterans. It started with my dad, an army corporal in World War II, and it continued with an elder brother who was a United States Marine infantryman in Vietnam and with my twenty-two years of service in the army, fulfilling my dad's desire for me to be the first military officer in the family. Now, my dad's grandson, the son of my elder brother, is the fourth generation of West combat veterans, a US Army major. The black community has raised men of color who stood for red, white, and blue even when those colors did not recognize them and their constitutional rights. It was just the right thing to do.

So, no, I do not need to respond when I am asked about being a black conservative. This book has taken us through a journey that asks the question at the end: Why are *you* not a conservative, if you are black? There can only be one response to my question—pure, unadulterated ignorance.

My hope is that this book will possibly stand the test of time and will one day take its place next to Booker T. Washington's *Up from Slavery*.

We can overcome, and this is my American black conservative manifesto.

Steadfast and loyal!
Lt. Col. Allen B. West (US Army, Ret.)
Member, 112th US Congress

ACKNOWLEDGMENTS

I want to acknowledge the highly professional and astute team at Brown Books Publishing Group, led by Milli Brown, with special thanks to Danny Whitworth for his memorable artistic design of our book cover. I pray that the images of these conservative black pioneers will never be forgotten.

My thanks to Jason Roberson for his dedication and incredible research ability. I also want to thank Brunella Costagliola for her impeccable editing of this, my third literary project.

But the true acknowledgment goes to the great American black conservative men and women who weathered the storm and through their insights, perspectives, and views made it possible for a fella like me born in Atlanta in a blacks-only hospital and raised in the historic Old Fourth Ward to grow to be considered a prominent black conservative voice in this time.

NOTES

INTRODUCTION

1. Project 21, "LBJ's 'War on Poverty' Hurt Black Americans," news release, National Center for Public Policy Research, January 8, 2014, https://nationalcenter.org/project21/2014/01/08/lbjs-war-on-poverty-hurt-black-americans/.

1. THE FOUNDATIONS OF THE ENSLAVED BLACK COMMUNITY

1. John T. Lanning, *Academic Culture in the Spanish Colonies* (New York: Oxford University Press, 1940).
2. Craig S. Wilder, *Ebony and Ivy* (New York: Bloomsbury Press, 2013).
3. Lanning, *Academic Culture in the Spanish Colonies.*
4. Marcia A. Smith, *Black America* (San Diego, California: Thunder Bay Press, 2002).
5. Smith, *Black America.*
6. Smith, *Black America.*
7. Wilder, *Ebony and Ivy.*
8. Wilder, *Ebony and Ivy.*
9. Smith, *Black America.*
10. Smith, *Black America.*
11. Wilder, *Ebony and Ivy.*
12. New-York Gazette, "The Diary of William Chancellor: A Ship's Doctor on Slaving Expedition to Africa, 1749–1751," *New-York Gazette*, May 13, 1751.
13. Wilder, *Ebony and Ivy.*
14. New-York Gazette, "The Diary of William Chancellor."
15. Wilder, *Ebony and Ivy*; Darold D. Wax, "Philadelphia Surgeon on a Slaving Voyage," *Pennsylvania History* (July 1965): 465–93.
16. Smith, *Black America.*
17. Walter Johnson, *Soul by Soul: Life Inside the Antebellum Slave Market* (Cambridge, Massachusetts: Harvard University Press, 1999).
18. Johnson, *Soul by Soul.*
19. Johnson, *Soul by Soul.*
20. Johnson, *Soul by Soul.*
21. Johnson, *Soul by Soul.*

22. Johnson, *Soul by Soul.*

23. Johnson, *Soul by Soul.*

24. Smith, *Black America.*

25. Smith, *Black America.*

26. Smith, *Black America.*

27. Johnson, *Soul by Soul.*

28. Johnson, *Soul by Soul.*

29. Johnson, *Soul by Soul.*

30. Johnson, *Soul by Soul.*

31. Johnson, *Soul by Soul.*

32. Johnson, *Soul by Soul.*

33. Johnson, *Soul by Soul.*

34. Johnson, *Soul by Soul.*

2. THE POLITICAL PARTY SCHISM ON THE ISSUE OF SLAVERY

1. Marcia A. Smith, *Black America* (San Diego, California: Thunder Bay Press, 2002).

2. Craig S. Wilder, *Ebony and Ivy* (New York: Bloomsbury Press, 2013).

3. Wilder, *Ebony and Ivy.*

4. Wilder, *Ebony and Ivy.*

5. Wilder, *Ebony and Ivy.*

6. Wilder, *Ebony and Ivy.*

7. Walter Johnson, *Soul by Soul: Life Inside the Antebellum Slave Market* (Cambridge, Massachusetts: Harvard University Press, 1999).

8. Johnson, *Soul by Soul.*

9. Johnson, *Soul by Soul.*

10. Johnson, *Soul by Soul.*

11. Johnson, *Soul by Soul.*

12. Johnson, *Soul by Soul.*

13. Johnson, *Soul by Soul.*

14. Johnson, *Soul by Soul.*

15. Martin Kelly, "What Were the Top 4 Causes of the Civil War?," ThoughtCo., accessed May 31, 2019, https://www.thoughtco.com/top-causes-of-the-civil-war-104532.

16. Robert McNamara, "The Great Irish Famine Was a Turning Point for Ireland and America," ThoughtCo., accessed April 13, 2019, https://www.thoughtco.com/great-irish-famine-1773826.

17. McNamara, "The Great Irish Famine Was a Turning Point for Ireland and America."

18. Kelly, "What Were the Top 4 Causes of the Civil War?"

19. Kelly, "What Were the Top 4 Causes of the Civil War?"

20. Kelly, "What Were the Top 4 Causes of the Civil War?"

21. Kelly, "What Were the Top 4 Causes of the Civil War?"

22. "Overview and History," Republican Party of Texas, accessed December 16, 2019, https://www.texasgop.org/overview-and-history/.

3. BLACK CONSERVATISM AND ITS EARLY CHAMPIONS

1. Janet Cornelius, "'We Slipped and Learned to Read': Slave Accounts of the Literacy Process, 1830–1865," *Phylon* 44, no. 3 (Third Quarter, 1983): 171, https://www.jstor.org/stable/274930?seq=1#page_scan_tab_contents.

2. "'To Redeem My Family': Venture Smith Frees Himself and his Family," History Matters, accessed September 7, 2019, http://historymatters.gmu.edu/d/6536/.

3. Eric Lincoln and Lawrence Mamiya, *The Black Church in the African American Experience* (Duke University Press, 1990), 251.

4. Lincoln, *The Black Church*, 251.

5. Laurie F. Maffly-Kipp, "An Introduction to the Church in the Southern Black Community," Documenting the American South, accessed September 1, 2019 https://docsouth.unc.edu/church/intro.html.

6. Lincoln, *The Black Church*, 243.

7. Frederick Douglass, "1888, Aug." (Frederick Douglass to men of Petersburg, VA, August 15, 1888), Frederick Douglass Papers at the Library of Congress, accessed December 16, 2019, http://hdl.loc.gov/loc.mss/mfd.07005.

8. Andrew Billingsley, *Yearning to Breathe Free: Robert Smalls of South Carolina and His Families* (Columbia, South Carolina: University of South Carolina Press, 2007), 38.

9. Patrick Brennan, *Secessionville: Assault on Charleston* (Savas Publishing, 1996).

10. Hagood Johnson, *Memoirs of the War of Secession* (State Company, 1910), https://books.google.com/books?id=yNVYAAAAMAAJ&pg=PA57#v=onepage&q&f=false.

11. Billingsley, *Yearning to Breathe Free*.

12. Howard Westwood, *Black Troops, White Commanders and Freedmen During the Civil War* (SIU Press, 1991).

13. Westwood, *Black Troops*.

14. Henry L. Gates, "100 Amazing Facts About the Negro: Which Slave Sailed Himself to Freedom?," PBS.org, 2013, http://www.pbs.org/wnet/african-americans-many-rivers-to-cross/history/which-slave-sailed-himself-to-freedom/.

15. Gates, "100 Amazing Facts About the Negro."

16. Gates, "100 Amazing Facts About the Negro."

17. Billingsley, *Yearning to Breathe Free*, 98.

18. "REVELS, Hiram Rhodes," History, Art & Archives, US House of Representatives, accessed July 14, 2019, https://history.house.gov/People/Listing/R/REVELS,-Hiram-Rhodes-(R000166)/.

19. Julius E. Thompson, "Hiram Rhodes Revels, 1827-1901: A Reappraisal." *Journal of Negro History* 79, no. 3 (1994): 297, doi:10.2307/2717508.

20. "REVELS, Hiram Rhodes."

21. Carter G. Woodson, *Autobiography of Hiram Revels* (Washington, DC: Library of Congress, 2019).

22. "REVELS, Hiram Rhodes."

23. "REVELS, Hiram Rhodes."

24. "REVELS, Hiram Rhodes."

25. "REVELS, Hiram Rhodes."

26. "REVELS, Hiram Rhodes."

27. "REVELS, Hiram Rhodes."

28. John Stauffer and Hendry Louis Gates, eds., *The Portable Frederick Douglass* (New York: Penguin Books, 2016), 37.

29. Frederick Douglass, "From the Archives: Frederick Douglass on the Republican Party," *Chicago Tribune*, January 29, 2015, https://www.chicagotribune.com/entertainment/books/ct-prj-archive-frederick-douglass-republican-party-20150129-story.html.

30. Frederick Douglass, "Frederick Douglass on the Republican Party."

31. Maud Cuney Hare, *Norris Wright Cuney: A Tribune of the Black People* (New York: Robert N. Wood, Printer, 1913), 82.

32. Merline Pitre, "Cuney, Norris Wright," Handbook of Texas Online, last modified July 7, 2016, http://www.tshaonline.org/handbook/online/articles/fcu20.

33. Pitre, "Cuney, Norris Wright."

34. Pitre, "Cuney, Norris Wright."

35. Alwyn Barr, "Black State Conventions," Handbook of Texas Online, last modified January 15, 2019, http://www.tshaonline.org/handbook/online/articles/pkb01.

36. Barr, "Black State Conventions."

37. Barr, "Black State Conventions."

38. Pitre, "Cuney, Norris Wright."

39. Pitre, "Cuney, Norris Wright."

40. Pitre, "Cuney, Norris Wright."

41. Paige Fry, "A Forgotten Obituary: Josiah T. Walls," Who Is Gainesville?, accessed September 21, 2019, https://whoisgainesville.com/obituary.

42. "WALLS, Josiah Thomas," History, Art & Archives, US House of Representatives, accessed July 15, 2019, https://history.house.gov/People/Detail/23324.

43. "WALLS, Josiah Thomas."

44. "WALLS, Josiah Thomas."

45. "WALLS, Josiah Thomas."

46. "WALLS, Josiah Thomas."

47. "WALLS, Josiah Thomas."

4. GAINS LOST AND THE RISE OF JIM CROW LAWS

1. "Race and Voting in the Segregated South," Constitutional Rights Foundation, accessed July 15, 2019, https://www.crf-usa.org/black-history-month/race-and-voting-in-the-segregated-south?xid=17259,1500008,15700023,15700043,15700105,15700124,15700149,15700168,15700173,15700186,15700201.

2. "Race and Voting in the Segregated South."

3. "Race and Voting in the Segregated South."

4. "Race and Voting in the Segregated South."

5. "Race and Voting in the Segregated South."

6. Charles W. Chesnutt, "The Disfranchisement of the Negro," in *The Negro Problem*, edited by Booker T. Washington (HardPress Publishing, 1903), 20–31.

7. Chesnutt, "The Disfranchisement of the Negro," 20–31.

8. Chesnutt, "The Disfranchisement of the Negro," 20–31.

9. Chesnutt, "The Disfranchisement of the Negro," 20–31.

5. THE FATHER OF BLACK CONSERVATISM: BOOKER T. WASHINGTON

1. Charles W. Chesnutt, "The Disfranchisement of the Negro," in *The Negro Problem*, edited by Booker T. Washington (HardPress Publishing, 1903), 20–31.

2. Booker T. Washington, "Industrial Education for the Negro," in *The Negro Problem*, edited by Booker T. Washington (HardPress Publishing, 1903), 3.

3. Washington, "Industrial Education for the Negro," 3.

4. W. E. B. Du Bois, "The Talented Tenth," in *The Negro Problem*, edited by Booker T. Washington (HardPress Publishing, 1903), 31–75.

5. Washington, "Industrial Education for the Negro," 3.

6. Washington, "Industrial Education for the Negro," 3.

7. A'Lelia Bundles, "Madam C. J. Walker: A Brief Biographical Essay," Madam C. J. Walker Official Web Site, accessed December 10, 2019, https://www.madamcjwalker.com/bios/madam-c-j-walker/.

6. "TO SUPPORT AND DEFEND . . ."

1. "1863: Military Service," Changing America, National Museum of American History, accessed December 16, 2019, https://americanhistory.si.edu/changing-america-emancipation-proclamation-1863-and-march-washington-1963/1863/military-service.

7. THE IDEOLOGICAL SHIFT OF THE BLACK COMMUNITY

1. Malcolm X, "God's Judgment of White America (The Chickens Come Home to Roost)" (speech, Manhattan Center, NY, December 1, 1963).

8. PRESIDENT TRUMAN AND THE DESEGREGATION OF THE ARMED FORCES

1. US Census Bureau, "Black Demographics," accessed March 25, 2019, https://blackdemographics.com/population/.
2. Harvard Sitkoff, *Toward Freedom Land: The Long Struggle for Racial Equality in America* (Kentucky: University Press of Kentucky, 2010), 39.
3. Sitkoff, *Toward Freedom Land*, 39.
4. Sitkoff, *Toward Freedom Land*, 40.
5. Quoted in Harvard Sitkoff, "Harry Truman and the Election of 1948: The Coming of Age of Civil Rights in American Politics," *Journal of Southern History* 37, no. 4 (November 1971): 597, http://doi.org/10.2307/2206548.
6. Jennifer Scanlon, *Until There Is Justice: The Life of Anna Arnold Hedgeman* (Oxford: Oxford University Press, 2016), 115.
7. Michael Gardner, *Harry Truman and Civil Rights: Moral Courage and Political Risks* (Southern Illinois University Press, 2002).
8. Gardner, *Harry Truman and Civil Rights*.
9. Gardner, *Harry Truman and Civil Rights*.
10. Gardner, *Harry Truman and Civil Rights*.
11. Gardner, *Harry Truman and Civil Rights*.
12. Gardner, *Harry Truman and Civil Rights*.
13. Henry Truman, "Address before the NAACP" (Washington, DC, National Archives, June 29, 1947).
14. Henry Truman, "Address before the NAACP."

15. Michael Ray, "Executive Order 9981," *Encyclopedia Britannica*, September 26, 2013.
16. Ray, "Executive Order 9981."
17. Ray, "Executive Order 9981."
18. Ray, "Executive Order 9981."
19. Ray, "Executive Order 9981."

9. PRESIDENT EISENHOWER CIVIL RIGHTS LEGACY

1. Adam Serwer, "Why Don't We Remember Ike as a Civil Rights Hero?," MSNBC.com, accessed April, 2019, http://www.msnbc.com/msnbc/why-dont-we-ike-civil-rights.
2. Serwer, "Why Don't We Remember Ike?"
3. Roy Wilkins, *Talking It Over with Roy Wilkins: Selected Speeches and Writings* (M&B Publishing Co., 1977).
4. "What Happened Next: President Eisenhower's Response," Facing History and Ourselves, n.d., https://www.facinghistory.org/resource-library/what-happened-next-president-eisenhowers-response.
5. Serwer, "Why Don't We Remember Ike?"
6. Leah Wright Rigueur, "When African-American Voters Shifted Away from the GOP," interview by Robert Siegel, *All Things Considered*, NPR, Politics, August 25, 2016, https://www.npr.org/2016/08/25/491389942/when-african-american-voters-shifted-away-from-the-gop.
7. Fredric Morrow, *Black Man in the White House: A Diary of the Eisenhower Years by the Administrative Officer for Special Projects, the White House, 1955–1961* (New York: Coward-McCann Inc., 1963), 98.
8. Morrow, *Black Man in the White House*, 98.

10. PRESIDENT KENNEDY AND THE NEW BLACK DEMOCRATS

1. Simeon Booker, *Shocking the Conscience: A Reporter's Account of the Civil Rights Movement* (Jackson: University Press of Mississippi, 2013).
2. Booker, *Shocking the Conscience*.
3. Booker, *Shocking the Conscience*.
4. Booker, *Shocking the Conscience*.
5. Booker, *Shocking the Conscience*.
6. Jesse Washington, "JFK Holds Complex Place in Black History," *San Diego Union-Tribune*, accessed August 31, 2019, https://www.sandiegouniontribune.com/sdut-jfk-holds-complex-place-in-black-history-2013nov03-story.html.

7.   "President John F. Kennedy's Civil Rights Legacy Is Complicated," Cleveland.com, US News, updated January 12, 2019, https://www. cleveland.com/nation/2013/02/president_john_f_kennedys_civi.html.

8.   Washington, "JFK Holds Complex Place in Black History."

9.   Taylor Branch, *Parting the Waters: America in the King Years 1954–63* (New York: Simon & Shuster, reprint edition, 1989), 840.

10. Booker, *Shocking the Conscience.*

11.   PRESIDENT JOHNSON'S OPPORTUNISTIC BEHAVIOR

1.   Robert Dallek, *Lone Star Rising: Lyndon Johnson and His Times* (New York City: Oxford University Press, 1991).

2.   Doris Kearns, *Lyndon Johnson and the American Dream* (New York: New American Library, 1977).

3.   Adam Serwer, "Lyndon Johnson Was a Civil Rights Hero. But Also a Racist," MSNBC.com, accessed April 23, 2019, http://www.msnbc.com/ msnbc/lyndon-johnson-civil-rights-racism.

4.   Serwer, "Lyndon Johnson Was a Civil Rights Hero."

5.   Harry J. Enten, "Were Republicans Really the Party of Civil Rights in the 1960s?," *Guardian*, accessed April 23, 2019, https://www.theguardian.com/ commentisfree/2013/aug/28/republicans-party-of-civil-rights.

6.   James Pethokoukis, "Tallying the Costs and Benefits of LBJ's Great Society," American Enterprise Institute, accessed May 11, 2019, https:// www.aei.org/economics/public-economics/tallying-the-costs-and- benefits-of-lbjs-great-society/.

7.   Edwin J. Feulner, "Assessing the 'Great Society,'" Heritage Foundation, accessed May 11, 2019, https://www.heritage.org/poverty-and- inequality/commentary/assessing-the-great-society.

8.   Project 21, "LBJ's 'War on Poverty' Hurt Black Americans," news release, National Center for Public Policy Research, January 8, 2014, https:// nationalcenter.org/project21/2014/01/08/lbjs-war-on-poverty-hurt- black-americans/.

12.   THE MOYNIHAN MINDSET

1.   James T. Patterson, "Moynihan and the Single-Parent Family," EducationNext, 2015, https://www.educationnext.org/moynihan-and- the-single-parent-family/.

2.   Patterson, "Moynihan and the Single-Parent Family."

3.   Patterson, "Moynihan and the Single-Parent Family."

4.   Patterson, "Moynihan and the Single-Parent Family."

5. Patterson, "Moynihan and the Single-Parent Family."

6. Daniel P. Moynihan, *The Negro Family: The Case for National Action* (Washington, DC: US Department of Labor, 1965).

7. Moynihan, *The Negro Family*.

8. Karl Gunnar Myrdal, *An American Dilemma: The Negro Problem and Modern Democracy* (New York: Harper and Row, 1944).

9. "Anatomy of White Guilt," Racial Equality Tools, accessed May 13, 2019, http://www.racialequitytools.org/resourcefiles/anatomy_white_guilt.pdf.

10. "Anatomy of White Guilt."

11. "Anatomy of White Guilt."

12. Moynihan, *The Negro Family*.

13. Thomas Sowell, *Is Reality Optional? And Other Essays* (Stanford, CA: Hoover Institution Press, 1993).

14. Patterson, "Moynihan and the Single-Parent Family."

15. Joseph Califano, "L.B.J. on Race Equality," *New York Times*, July 3, 2003.

16. "LBJ's 'War on Poverty' Hurt Black Americans."

17. Alan Brinkley, "Great Society," in *The Reader's Companion to American History*, edited by E. F. Garraty (Houghton Mifflin Books), 472.

18. James Piereson, "A Not-So-Great Society," *Washington Examiner*, accessed May 4, 2019, https://www.weeklystandard.com/james-piereson/a-not-so-great-society.

19. Piereson, "A Not-So-Great Society."

20. Piereson, "A Not-So-Great Society."

13. PRESIDENT NIXON'S SUPPORT TO INTEGRATE

1. Richard Nixon, "1969 Inaugural Speech Initial Drafts," Richard Nixon Foundation, accessed May 14, 2019, https://www.nixonfoundation.org/2019/01/1969-inaugural-speech-initial-drafts/.

2. "Nixon's Record on Civil Rights," Richard Nixon Foundation, August 4, 2017, https://www.nixonfoundation.org/2017/08/nixons-record-civil-rights-2/.

3. "Nixon's Record on Civil Rights."

4. "Nixon's Record on Civil Rights."

5. "Nixon's Record on Civil Rights."

6. "Nixon's Record on Civil Rights."

7. "Nixon's Record on Civil Rights."

8. "Nixon's Record on Civil Rights."

14. PRESIDENT CARTER AND THE COMMUNITY REINVESTMENT ACT

1. "The Effectiveness of the Community Reinvestment Act," Congressional Research Service, accessed May 14, 2019, https://fas.org/sgp/crs/misc/R43661.pdf.

2. Kimberly Amadeo, "What Caused the Subprime Mortgage Crisis," The Balance, accessed May 19, 2019, https://www.thebalance.com/what-caused-the-subprime-mortgage-crisis-3305696.

3. Amadeo, "What Caused the Subprime Mortgage Crisis."

4. Amadeo, "What Caused the Subprime Mortgage Crisis."

5. "The Effectiveness of the Community Reinvestment Act."

6. "The Effectiveness of the Community Reinvestment Act."

7. "The Effectiveness of the Community Reinvestment Act."

15. BLACK LIVES MATTER . . . WHICH ONES?

1. Michael Cooper, "Officers in Bronx Fire 41 Shots, and an Unarmed Man Is Killed," *New York Times*, February 5, 1999.

2. Cooper, "Officers in Bronx Fire 41 Shots."

3. Jane Fritsch, "The Diallo Verdict: The Overview," *New York Times*, February 26, 2000.

4. Fritsch, "The Diallo Verdict: The Overview."

5. Cooper, "Officers in Bronx Fire 41 Shots, And an Unarmed Man Is Killed."

6. Julia Craven, "Black Lives Matter Co-Founder Reflects on the Origins of the Movement," *Huffington Post*, September 30, 2015, https://www.huffpost.com/entry/black-lives-matter-opal-tometi_n_560c1c59e4b0768127003227.

7. Ryan Miller, "Black Lives Matter: A Primer on What It Is and What It Stands For," *USA Today*, updated August 8, 2016, https://www.usatoday.com/story/news/nation/2016/07/11/black-lives-matter-what-what-stands/86963292/.

8. Craven, "Black Lives Matter Co-Founder Reflects."

9. John Blake, "Is Black Lives Matter Blowing It?," CNN, updated August 2, 2016, http://www.cnn.com/2016/07/29/us/black-lives-matter-blowing-it/.

10. Miller, "Black Lives Matter."

11. Jelani Cobb, "The Matter of Black Lives," *New Yorker*, March 6, 2016, https://www.newyorker.com/magazine/2016/03/14/where-is-black-lives-matter-headed.

12. Miller, "Black Lives Matter."

13. James Simpson, "Black Lives Matter," Capital Research Center, September 21, 2016, https://capitalresearch.org/article/blm-roots/.

14. V. Richardson, "Black Lives Matter Cashes In with $100 Million from Liberal Foundations," *Washington Times*, August 16, 2016.

15. Jeremy Borden, Sari Horwitz, and Jerry Markon, "From Victims' Families, Forgiveness for Accused Charleston Gunman Dylann Roof," *Washington Post*, June 19, 2015, https://www.washingtonpost.com/politics/south-carolina-governor-urges-death-penalty-charges-in-church-slayings/2015/06/19/3c039722-1678-11e5-9ddc-e3353542100c_story.html.

16. Jason Kopp, "'Ferguson Effect' Legit? Police Laud FBI Report That Says Cop Killings 'New Norm,'" Fox News, updated April 25, 2018, http://www.foxnews.com/us/2017/05/12/ferguson-effect-legit-police-laud-fbi-report-that-says-cop-killings-new-norm.html.

17. Madison Park, "Black Lives Matter Protesters Return to the Streets," CNN, updated July 9, 2016, http://www.cnn.com/2016/07/09/us/black-lives-matter-protests/index.html.

18. Martin Kaste, "Shortage of Officers Fuels Police Recruiting Crisis," National Public Radio, December 11, 2018, https://www.npr.org/2018/12/11/675505052/shortage-of-officers-fuels-police-recruiting-crisis.

19. Kaste, "Shortage of Officers Fuels Police Recruiting Crisis."

20. Kaste, "Shortage of Officers Fuels Police Recruiting Crisis."

21. "In Chicago, 171 people have been killed this year," *Chicago Tribune*, May 18, 2019.

22. "In Chicago, 171 people have been killed this year."

23. "In Chicago, 171 people have been killed this year."

24. "Abortion Is the Biggest Single Negative Force on Black American Growth," Urban Cure, April 30, 2018, https://www.urbancure.org/blog/post/abortion-is-the-biggest-single-negative-force-on-black-american-growth.

16. THE DECIMATION OF THE TRADITIONAL BLACK FAMILY

1. Annie E. Casey Foundation, "Children in Single-Parent Families by Race in the United States," Kids Count Data Center, updated March 2019, https://datacenter.kidscount.org/data/tables/107-children-in-single-parent-families-by-race#detailed/1/any/false/871,870,573,869,36,868,867,133,38,35/10,11,9,12,1,185,13/432,431.

2. Annie E. Case Foundation, "Children in Single-Parent Families."

3. Tami Luhby, "This Group Is Getting Ahead in America," CNNMoney, June 22, 2018, https://money.cnn.com/2018/06/22/news/economy/hispanic-social-mobility/index.html.

4. Luhby, "This Group Is Getting Ahead in America."

5. Luhby, "This Group Is Getting Ahead in America."

6. "Poverty in Black America," Black Demographics, https:// blackdemographics.com/households/poverty/.

7. Daniel P. Moynihan, *The Negro Family: The Case for National Action* (Washington DC: US Department of Labor, 1965).

8. *National Review*, April 4, 1994, 24.

9. Jesse Washington, "Blacks Struggle with 72 Percent Unwed Mothers Rate," NBC News, updated November 7, 2010, http://www.nbcnews. com/id/39993685/ns/health-womens_health/t/blacks-struggle-percent- unwed-mothers-rate/#.XWFinuhKjIU; Paul Bedard, "77% Black Births to Single Moms, 49% for Hispanic Immigrants," *Washington Examiner*, May 5, 2017, https://www.washingtonexaminer.com/77-black-births-to- single-moms-49-for-hispanic-immigrants.

10. Philip A. Klinkner and Rogers M. Smith, *The Unsteady March: The Rise and Decline of Racial Equality in America* (University of Chicago Press, 2002).

11. "Black Veterans Return From World War II," SNCC Digital, n.d., https://snccdigital.org/events/black-veterans-return-from-world-war-ii/.

12. United States Census Bureau, "21.3 Percent of U.S. Population Participates in Government Assistance Programs Each Month," news release no. CB15- 97, May 28, 2015, https://www.census.gov/newsroom/press-releases/2015/ cb15-97.html.

13. Lexington Law, "45 Important Welfare for 2019," *Credit Advice* (blog), December 31, 2018, https://www.lexingtonlaw.com/blog/finance/ welfare-statistics.html.

14. Moynihan, *The Negro Family*.

17. WHERE ARE THE SMALL BUSINESSES?

1. Michael McManus, "Minority Business Ownership," *Issue Brief*, no.12 (September 14, 2016), https://www.sba.gov/sites/default/files/advocacy/ Minority-Owned-Businesses-in-the-US.pdf.

2. McManus, "Minority Business Ownership."

3. McManus, "Minority Business Ownership."

4. McManus, "Minority Business Ownership."

5. McManus, "Minority Business Ownership."

6. McManus, "Minority Business Ownership."

7. McManus, "Minority Business Ownership."

8. McManus, "Minority Business Ownership."

9. "Sweet Auburn Historic District," National Park Service, https://www. nps.gov/nr/travel/atlanta/aub.htm.

10. "Sweet Auburn Historic District."

11. J. H. Haley, "Black Dixie: Afro-Texan History and Culture in Houston," *Georgia Historical Quarterly*, (1993): 412–13.

12. Tyina Steptoe, "Fifth Ward, Houston, Texas (1866–)," BlackPast, April 19, 2015, https://www.blackpast.org/african-american-history/fifth-ward-houston-texas-1866/.

13. Steptoe, "Fifth Ward."

14. Steptoe, "Fifth Ward."

15. Mandy, "The Race Riot That Destroyed Black Wall Street," Official Black Wall Street, July 22, 2015, https://officialblackwallstreet.com/black-wall-street-story/.

16. Mandy, "The Race Riot That Destroyed Black Wall Street."

17. Mandy, "The Race Riot That Destroyed Black Wall Street."

18. Mandy, "The Race Riot That Destroyed Black Wall Street."

19. McManus, "Minority Business Ownership."

20. McManus, "Minority Business Ownership."

21. C. Le, "Asian Small Businesses," Asian Nation: The Landscape of Asian America, 2019, http://www.asian-nation.org/small-business.shtml#sthash.3WPTAWFh.0doi3Jnl.dpbs.

22. Le, "Asian Small Businesses."

23. Alicia Robb and Arnobio Morelix, "Startup Financing Trends by Race: How Access to Capital Impacts Profitability," Ewing Marion Kauffman Foundation, October 27, 2016.

24. Robb and Morelix, "Startup Financing Trends by Race."

25. Le, "Asian Small Businesses."

26. Le, "Asian Small Businesses."

18. SEPARATE AND UNEQUAL: EDUCATION IN AMERICA

1. Ary Spatig-Amerikaner, "Unequal Education: Federal Loophole Enables Lower Spending on Students of Color," Center for American Progress, August 2012, https://www.uncf.org/wp-content/uploads/PDFs/UnequalEduation.pdf.

2. Gary Orfield, "Reviving the Goal of an Integrated Society: A 21st Century Challenge," Civil Rights Project at UCLA (Los Angeles, 2009).

3. Spatig-Amerikaner, "Unequal Education."

4. Spatig-Amerikaner, "Unequal Education."

5. Spatig-Amerikaner, "Unequal Education."

6. Spatig-Amerikaner, "Unequal Education."

7. Spatig-Amerikaner, "Unequal Education."

8. Spatig-Amerikaner, "Unequal Education."

9. "Brown v. Board at Fifty: 'With an Even Hand,'" Library of Congress, https://www.loc.gov/exhibits/brown/brown-segregation.html.

10. "Brown v. Board at Fifty."

11. "Brown v. Board at Fifty."

12. "Brown v. Board at Fifty."

13. Jeannette Smyth, "The Education of Shirley Mount Hufstedler," *Washington Post*, January 27, 1980.

14. Smyth, "The Education of Shirley Mount Hufstedler."

15. Smyth, "The Education of Shirley Mount Hufstedler."

16. Smyth, "The Education of Shirley Mount Hufstedler."

17. Smyth, "The Education of Shirley Mount Hufstedler."

18. Anthony Fisher, "Why Do We Have a Department of Education? Jimmy Carter's Debt to a Teachers Union," Reason, February 7, 2017, https://reason.com/2017/02/07/department-of-education-jimmy-carter/.

19. Shayla L. Mitchell, "A Historical Analysis of the Creation of a Cabinet-Level Department of Education," Georgia State University, May 16, 2008, https://scholarworks.gsu.edu/cgi/viewcontent.cgi?referer=&httpsredir=1&article=1021&context=eps_diss.

20. "Cato Handbook for Congress," Cato Institute, n.d., https://object.cato.org/sites/cato.org/files/serials/files/cato-handbook-policymakers/2003/9/hb108-28.pdf.

21. Marcus Hawkins, "How Conservatives Would Reform Education," Thought Co., updated April 2, 2018, https://www.thoughtco.com/how-conservatives-would-reform-education-3303567.

22. Hawkins, "How Conservatives Would Reform Education."

23. Hawkins, "How Conservatives Would Reform Education."

24. Hawkins, "How Conservatives Would Reform Education."

25. Hawkins, "How Conservatives Would Reform Education."

26. "Cato Handbook for Congress."

27. "Cato Handbook for Congress."

28. "Cato Handbook for Congress."

29. "Cato Handbook for Congress."

30. "Cato Handbook for Congress"; "Budget fact sheet," US Department of Education, n.d., https://www2.ed.gov/about/overview/budget/budget17/budget-factsheet.pdf.

31. National Center for Education Statistics, "Status and Trends in the Education of Racial and Ethnic Groups," US Department of Education, 2017.

32. "Status and Trends in the Education of Racial and Ethnic Groups."

33. "Status and Trends in the Education of Racial and Ethnic Groups."

34. "Status and Trends in the Education of Racial and Ethnic Groups."

35. US Department of Education Office for Civil Rights, "Data Snapshot: College and Career Readiness," US Department of Education, Issue Brief no. 3 (March 21, 2014), https://www.uncf.org/wp-content/uploads/PDFs/CRDC-College-and-Career-Readiness-Snapshot-2.pdf.

36. "Data Snapshot."

37. "Data Snapshot."

38. "Data Snapshot."

39. "Data Snapshot."

40. "Data Snapshot."

41. "Data Snapshot."

42. "Data Snapshot."

43. United Negro College Fund, "The Condition of College & Career Readiness 2015: African American Students," ACT Inc., https://www.uncf.org/wp-content/uploads/PDFs/6201-CCCR-African-American-2015.pdf.

44. "Conservative Principles Essential to US Education," Conservative Leaders for Education, https://conservativeleaders4ed.org/conservative-principles-essential-to-u-s-education/.

45. "Conservative Principles."

19. THE RISE OF BLACK PROGRESSIVE SOCIALISM AND TODAY'S TALENTED TENTH

1. Henry Lyman Morehouse, "The Talented Tenth," *American Missionary* 50, no. 6 (June 1896), Project Gutenburg Ebook (2006), http://www.gutenberg.org/files/19890/19890-0.txt.

2. W. E. B. Du Bois, "The Talented Tenth," in *The Negro Problem*, edited by Booker T. Washington (HardPress Publishing, 1903), 31–75.

3. Ibram X. Kendi, "Colorism as Racism: Garvey, Du Bois and the Other Color Line," Black Perspectives, May 24, 2017, https://www.aaihs.org/colorism-as-racism-garvey-du-bois-and-the-other-color-line/.

4. Kendi, "Colorism as Racism."

5. Kendi, "Colorism as Racism."

6. Kendi, "Colorism as Racism."

7. Kendi, "Colorism as Racism."

8. *I Am Not Your Negro*, directed by Raoul Peck, written by James Baldwin and Raoul Peck, featuring Samuel L. Jackson (Los Angeles, CA: Magnolia Home Entertainment, 2017), widescreen video recording, 94 min.

9. "Application to Join the CPUSA by W.E.B. Du Bois, 1961," Communist Party USA, February 28, 2009, https://www.cpusa.org/party_info/application-to-join-the-cpusa-by-w-e-b-du-bois-1961/.

10. Marian L. Tupy, "Anti-Racists Should Think Twice about Allying with Socialism," Foundation for Economic Education, November 14, 2017, https://fee.org/articles/anti-racists-should-think-twice-about-allying-with-socialism/#0.

11. Tupy, "Anti-Racists Should Think Twice about Allying with Socialism."

12. Tupy, "Anti-Racists Should Think Twice about Allying with Socialism."

20. ECONOMIC RESURGENCE OF THE BLACK COMMUNITY

1. Dedrick Asante-Muhammed et al., "The Ever-Growing Gap," Institute for Policy Studies, August 2016, https://ips-dc.org/wp-content/uploads/2016/08/The-Ever-Growing-Gap-CFED_IPS-Final-2.pdf.

2. Asante-Muhammed, "The Ever-Growing Gap."

3. Asante-Muhammed, "The Ever-Growing Gap."

4. Algernon Austin, "A Jobs-Centered Approach to African American Community Development," Economic Policy Institute, December 14, 2011, https://www.epi.org/publication/bp328-african-american-unemployment/#_ednref4.

5. Austin, "A Jobs-Centered Approach."

6. Austin, "A Jobs-Centered Approach."

7. Austin, "A Jobs-Centered Approach."

8. Austin, "A Jobs-Centered Approach."

9. Austin, "A Jobs-Centered Approach."

10. Austin, "A Jobs-Centered Approach."

11. Sylvia Allegretto and Steven Pitts, "The State of Black Workers before the Great Recession," Berkeley, California: UC Berkeley Labor Center, 2010.

12. Harry Alford, "Beyond the Rhetoric," National Black Chamber of Commerce, n.d., https://www.nationalbcc.org/news/beyond-the-rhetoric/251-beyond-the-rhetoric-40.

13. Ashley Fox, "Blacks are Financially Struggling: Here's How We Can Help Them," *Forbes*, December 7, 2018, https://www.forbes.com/sites/ashleymfox/2018/12/07/blacks-are-financially-struggling-heres-how-we-can-help-them/#4c4c090f6a0b.

14. Willy Foote, "How to Build a Public-Private Partnership That's More Than a Marriage of Convenience," *Forbes*, November 29, 2017, https://www.forbes.com/sites/willyfoote/2017/11/29/how-to-build-public-private-partnership/#6fd728154bfa.

15. Foote, "How to Build a Public-Private Partnership."

16. "The Need," Prison Entrepreneurship Program, https://www.pep.org/the-problem-need/.

17. "The Need."

18. "The Need."

19. "Results," Prison Entrepreneurship Program, https://www.pep.org/pep-results/.

20. "Results."

21. "The Need."

22. "The Need."

23. Daniel P. Moynihan, *The Negro Family: The Case for National Action* (Washington, DC: US Department of Labor, 1965).

CONCLUSION

1. Project 21, "LBJ's 'War on Poverty' Hurt Black Americans," news release, National Center for Public Policy Research, January 8, 2014, https://nationalcenter.org/project21/2014/01/08/lbjs-war-on-poverty-hurt-black-americans/.

ABOUT THE AUTHOR

Lt. Col. Allen West (Ret.) believes it will be principled constitutional conservative policies, not politics, which secure a sound economic future for Americans—with growth, opportunity, and a return to the promise of the American dream for this generation and those to come.

Lt. Col. West is the third of four generations of military servicemen in his family. During his twenty-two year career in the United States Army, West served in several combat zones and received many honors, including a Bronze Star, three Meritorious Service Medals, three Army Commendation Medals, one with Valor device, and a Valorous Unit Award. In 1993 he was named the US Army ROTC Instructor of the Year.

In November of 2010, Allen was elected to the United States Congress, representing Florida's 22nd District. As a member of the 112th Congress, he sat on the Small Business and Armed Services Committees and was instrumental in passage of the 2011 and 2012 National Defense Authorization Acts.

West is a Fox News contributor, senior fellow of the Media Research Center, former director of the Booker T. Washington Initiative (BTWI) for the Texas Public Policy Foundation, and former executive director of the National Center for Policy Analysis in Dallas, Texas.

A commissioned officer in the Texas State Guard, West is also a legacy life member of the Veterans of Foreign Wars, life member of the American Legion, life member of the Association of the United States Army, the Society of the First Infantry Division, 4th Infantry Division, and 101st Airborne Division. He is a Patriot life member (benefactor) and board of directors' member of the National Rifle Association and a life member (benefactor) of the Texas State Rifle Association.

Lieutenant Colonel West is an inductee into the University of Tennessee Army ROTC Hall of Fame. He serves on the board of advisors of Amegy Bank, Dallas region, and in 2016, Lt. Col. West was appointed by Texas Lt. Gov. Dan Patrick to the Texas Sunset Advisory Commission.

West is an avid distance runner, a master scuba diver, and a motorcyclist, and in his spare time he enjoys cheering his beloved Tennessee Volunteers.

We Can Overcome: An American Black Conservative Manifesto is West's third book, after *Guardian of the Republic: An American Ronin's Journey to Family, Faith and Freedom* and *Hold Texas, Hold the Nation: Victory or Death.*

Allen West is married to Dr. Angela Graham-West. They have two grown daughters, Aubrey and Austen, and live in Garland, Texas.